Caring
for your
Aging Parent

A Guide for Catholic Families

Monica & Bill Dodds

Our Sunday Visitor Publishing Division
Our Sunday Visitor, Inc.
Huntington, Indiana 46750

Some of the material in this book has been published in the family columns Bill and Monica Dodds write for the Catholic News Service and the Knights of Columbus' *Columbia* magazine and in articles in *Catholic Digest* magazine. If any copyrighted materials have been inadvertently used in this work without the proper credit being given, please notify Our Sunday Visitor in writing so that future printings of this work may be corrected accordingly.

International Standard Book Number: 0-87973-731-X
Library of Congress Catalog Card Number: 97-66311

Cover design by Monica Watts

PRINTED IN THE UNITED STATES OF AMERICA

731

Dedication

In loving memory of our grandparents:

John and Lora Faudree
Bernard and Mary Gallagher
Charles and Margaret Farrell
John and Jeannette Dodds

Contents

The Caregiver's Life

On Death and Dying

Appendixes

Caring for Your Aging Parent: A Guide for Catholic Families

Introduction: How to Use This Book

If you're an adult child working with your aging parent, you probably have very little time and even less energy. That's why we've written eighty short chapters that can be read in any order.

We suggest you zero in on the chapter or two most relevant to your particular circumstances right now. We know that your needs and concerns, and those of your parent, don't follow any textbook formula.

Right now, your focus may be on the losses, the many things your parent has been forced to give up in recent years. A little later, it may be dealing with your siblings, who have a very different idea of what Mom or Dad needs. Later still, the issue may be guilt, when it seems that no matter what you do — or don't do — you feel at fault.

Please keep in mind that this book wasn't designed to add to your feelings of guilt. We know that if your daily schedule includes responsibilities with a family, work, and an aging parent, it will take some juggling just to arrange the five or ten minutes or so it will take to read one chapter.

We're not offering simple answers to the complicated challenges you face. These are suggestions, food for thought, that can be adapted to fit your circumstances.

Also, we want to make it clear this book isn't written just for adult children and aging parents. It's for anyone taking care of a loved one. Although we use the terms "adult children" and "aging parent" and focus on that particular relationship, the same material may be adapted and applied if you're taking care of a spouse, a grandparent, an aunt or uncle, a sibling, or any other family member or friend.

We hope, too, that the information and suggestions we're offering will be of value to "professional caregivers," those whose jobs — whose vocations — make such a difference in so many people's lives.

Some underlying principles

You'll notice throughout "Caring for Your Aging Parent" some underlying principles are repeated. When you, the caregiver, are facing a particular issue or concern, it may be helpful to keep these principles in mind. Consider how your idea, plan, or solution corresponds — or doesn't correspond — with:

•**Love and respect:** No matter how old you and your parent are, the lifetime bond between you is like no other. As an adult, you probably realize that this relationship is seldom ideal and never perfect, and yet it is a tremendously important factor. As the adult child of an aging parent, you're now being given the opportunity — the challenge — to "honor" your mother and father in a new, different and more demanding way.

•**Self-determination:** It's still your *parent's* life, not yours. You're there to assist, not take over. As long as your parent is mentally competent, he or she should be included in decisions and their choices should be respected.

•**Normalization:** A basic goal for you is to help your parent continue to lead the same lifestyle he or she has been leading and wants to keep leading (provided, of course, that lifestyle is not undermining his or her health or safety). The challenge is to begin with the minimum amount of help or change that's necessary, and then, as needed, gradually increase it.

•**Communication:** Planning early and talking often, even about difficult subjects, will help you and your parent avoid having to work things out in the middle of a crisis.

•**Support:** A number of support systems are available for both you and your aging parent. In addition to family, friends, neighbors, and members of the parish, both professional and peer-group systems of support can be extremely helpful.

•**Ongoing process:** The aging process never stops, and each step along the way brings new challenges for both you and your parent. As your parent's health deteriorates, your traditional roles as adult and child — the one who has always provided the help and the one who needed that help — may continue to fluctuate or reverse. These changes are new for both of you and may seem overwhelming. Remember, neither you nor your parent has to be an expert. You can learn, together.

•**Solutions:** Most often there are no quick fixes to your parent's increasing needs, no simple answers. Keep in mind that even the best solution is only temporary. As your parent's situation changes, and it will, even the best answer will have to be reviewed and reworked.

Emotions run high

Throughout "Caring for Your Aging Parent," you will be encouraged to consider the emotions you're feeling — anger, fear, worry, grief, and so on — and to realize your mother or father has similar feelings but for very different reasons. Your emotions may not match. Mom is grieving because so many of her friends have died, and you're feeling guilty about not spending enough time with your spouse and children. Dad is afraid of his upcoming surgery, and you're angry that Medicare regulations seem so complicated.

What each of you face is not easy. There is no way to avoid these feelings. Our goal is to help you acknowledge these feelings, realize they're normal, and to offer you some tips for coping with them.

When we write about physical, mental, emotional, social and spiritual needs, we're writing about your needs as well as your parent's. While this book was written primarily for you, the caregiver, it is of value to your siblings who are not the front-line caregivers.

If both of your parents are living, "Caring for Your Aging

Parent" can help your healthy parent better understand and acknowledge what is happening.

Information on medical, financial and legal issues is offered strictly from a lay person's point of view. We hope to help you ask the questions while offering suggestions for where to turn to learn more. **We are not giving medical, financial, or legal advice**. Please consult a physician or other health-care professional, financial advisor or lawyer for help with your particular concerns.

A time to pray

We begin each chapter with a brief prayer. This is to help you pause for a moment to take a deep breath and turn to an all-loving God, to ask for help in your role as caregiver, and to give thanks for this parent who means so much to you.

One point along the way

Caring for an aging parent can be bewildering because it all seems so new and strange. At each stage of your life — as a preschooler, grade-schooler, adolescent, young adult, and adult — the relationship between you and your parent changed as you both adapted to the realities of growing up, growing older. The same is true now.

As an adult child caring for an aging parent, you are at another point along that same continuum. In many ways, this will be the most demanding point for each of you, but it can also be the most rewarding. This can be a time to draw closer, to take advantage of the opportunity to say "I love you and thank God for you." A chance to say good-bye.

The Realities of Growing Older

Dear God, time is just passing too fast and it scares me. Help me to accept your time line.

1. "Not *My* Parent"

This is different. Of course your parent is getting older. Everybody is getting older. Everybody dies. But this isn't "everybody." This is *your* parent.

You're not the only one who feels this way. Many members of the baby-boomer generation, who crowded playgrounds and classrooms, work places and housing markets, are facing the undeniable fact that as they enter middle age, their parents are marking their seventieth, eightieth, or even ninetieth birthdays.

And suddenly — it always seems suddenly — the people who cared and nurtured and taught and provided are the ones who need help. Suddenly Mom isn't as independent as she used to be. Suddenly Dad is letting slide tasks he's been handling faithfully for more than half a century.

The realization that a parent needs help isn't an intellectual exercise. It is a realization that gnaws at the heart and begins with self-doubt. Soon after, guilt, panic, frustration, and grief fight for dominance.

If you're an adult child living near your aging parent, you probably blame yourself for not noticing the gradual deterioration. Maybe Mom had a small stroke and fell and stayed on the kitchen floor all night until a neighbor happened to stop by. Why haven't you dropped in more often? Why did it take something big?

If you live in another part of the country, a visit home to see Dad —
a visit you've put off for how long? — may be shocking. The small
and not-so-small changes and problems have added up, and the
spunky, independent person you remember is no longer there. Why
didn't you come sooner? Why didn't you notice the difference when
the two of you spoke by phone? Why wasn't it obvious his letters
were more muddled and arrived less frequently? Why did you take
that job so far away?

No wonder you start to feel panicky. You need to solve these
problems *now!*

But you can't. In fact, you shouldn't.

First, you can't solve *all* the problems *now.* Your parent didn't
reach this condition overnight, and it will take time to make changes.
There are no quick fixes.

Second, *you* — singular — shouldn't solve the problems. If you
swoop in and begin giving orders, you may be not so pleasantly
surprised to see that the proud, self-reliant (some might say stubborn
and cantankerous) person you thought gone is not gone entirely. Not
by a long shot.

The more your parent is involved in finding solutions to the
problems, the more cooperative he or she will be. The fancy name for
this is "self-determination." It's really common sense. Sometimes,
and understandably so, common sense gives way to guilt and panic.

And then there's the frustration. Why does it take a dozen
phone calls to find the right agency to deliver the service your parent
needs? Why do you always feel as if you're either not doing enough
or you're doing too much? Why don't you have the energy or time or
money to properly take care of your spouse, your kids, and your
parent?

In the dead of night, grief wins. There's the icy realization that
your parent is going to die. As you try to cope and solve and assist,
you can't help feeling this is the beginning of the end. You can't help
the grief you feel because you know someday your mother or father
will be gone.

You lie there and pray, "Please, God, not yet. Not *my* parent."

Lord, sometimes I just don't know what to think. Help me find the information I need so I can do what's best for my parent.

2. Should You Blame It on Aging?

Is your parent developing a new and potentially serious health problem, or is it simply part of what could be called the natural aging process? How are you supposed to tell the difference?

Throughout our lives, our bodies change. Even members of the middle generation know about aging. Just how quickly those wrinkles appear, the gray hair comes in, those tired eyes need reading glasses depends in part on our genes and lifestyle. As long as a human body is living, it is growing older.

The temptation is to assume that a new problem your parent develops is one every older person experiences and nothing can be done about it. Not necessarily.

Take being confused, for example. Aren't a lot of elderly people more forgetful than they used to be? Doesn't everyone, if he or she lives long enough, have problems with mild dementia?

Medical research now says, yes, the chances of developing Alzheimer's disease increase with age, but there are other reasons a parent might be suffering from confusion. Maybe Dad's metabolism has changed and a medicine he's taken for years is causing side effects. Or perhaps the problem is a new medicine combined with what he's already taking. Maybe, without your knowledge, Mom is drinking more than she used to. Maybe she has had a small stroke.

This is why it's a good idea is to ask your parent's primary physician about the "normal" aging process — what, in general, is to be expected — and keep the doctor up to date on what's happening with your mother or father. If you see something new, ask the doctor.

Also, keep in mind:

•It's a good idea to consult with the physician even if you think what you see is to be expected with any chronic condition your parent may have. (And it's important for you to know the usual progression of that condition.) Say, for example, Mom has arthritis and she's having more pain and more difficulty using her hands.

Isn't that the nature of arthritis?

Yes, it may be inevitable her condition will grow worse, but perhaps a more effective medicine or treatment will help as the inflammation reaches this new stage. Is physical therapy available that would help her feel better? Would occupational therapy or one of the many adaptive devices available make it easier for her to perform daily tasks like holding a fork or using a zipper? Ask.

•Don't compare your parent's condition or symptoms with another older person's. Maybe your best friend noticed her father was growing hard of hearing and now he wears a hearing aid. You notice your father's hearing isn't what it used to be, but you hesitate to bring up the subject with Dad or his doctor because you're fairly certain getting your parent to accept a hearing aid would be a tremendous battle.

At the same time, Dad, who has noticed the trouble he's having, is too frightened to say anything. And he's worried.

While you both tiptoe around the subject, the source of your father's problem may be nothing more than wax building up in his ears. His doctor's nurse could quickly and easily take care of it and give both of you tips on how to avoid the problem in the future.

•Don't assume what you see happening to your parent is only the latest in a series of what has already been happening. Yes, it could be. On the other hand, another condition or problem could have an identical symptom. Again, always run your concerns by your parent's doctor.

Remember that while you and your parent may become very good at spotting and diagnosing a change or a problem, that's not the same as having an objective health-care professional evaluate what's happening. Let that person be the one to decide if it's an inevitable part of the aging process.

Society and the Elderly

Dear Father, respect for the elderly starts right here, right now with my parent. Help me put my beliefs into practice.

3. Respect for the Elderly

Different cultures have different attitudes toward the elderly. Some consider their senior members treasures of wisdom — a true blessing; others believe they're useless has-beens — an economic burden.

Unfortunately, our society in general continues to lean toward the latter view. There are constant threats on the political front to cut programs and services designed to assist our elderly. While members of the younger generations may be concerned about their own later years, their self-concern doesn't necessarily translate into wanting to — or seeing a need to — provide care for today's older citizens.

In a society that idolizes youth, independence, and productivity, it isn't surprising that the elderly become targets. That they, and their needs, are seen as a drain on the public coffers.

On a more personal level, we don't always do a good job of teaching our children basic manners when it comes to their elders. There are many children who don't know they're supposed to stand when a member of the senior generation enters the room, or that they're supposed to call an elderly person who's not a relative by his or her surname ("Mr. Johnson" or "Mrs. Sanchez") unless that person requests otherwise.

Part of our responsibility to "honor" our fathers and mothers, to quote the fourth commandment, is to teach our children, by our words and by our actions, what "honor" means. Another part of our responsibility is to keep an eye out when talks of cuts in government services for the elderly surface and to make sure our views are heard.

To honor, to respect, our elders is one of the founding blocks of who we are as Catholics. The first three commandments have to do with our relationship to God. The next one talks about our parents, our elders. It's that important. That central.

How do you "honor" your parent at this stage in the relationship the two of you share? You offer *compassionate* care — not simply feeding or bathing or dressing Mom or Dad but doing so in a gentle, loving way. In a way that isn't threatening. That isn't abusive. Any form of abuse is a clear sign outside help is needed. *(See "Reporting Abuse" in the back of the book.)*

This is the attitude you should have as you make sure the apartment is clean. That the bills are paid and the checkbook balances. That the doctor appointments are made and kept.

You honor your parent by giving Mom choices and control over her life. By helping Dad have a lifestyle that's as close to "normal," as close to what he really wants, as his illness, disability or condition will allow.

You honor your parent by giving age-appropriate care. You don't treat your parent like a child or a baby even if dementia or illness has affected his or her mental and/or physical abilities.

Most of all, you honor your parent by treating him or her with dignity and with respect. They're two aspects of the multi-faceted love you share. Two fundamental aspects.

Our society is quickly forgetting how to honor its senior members. But through the example set by you and others like you in similar situations, all of us are reminded of what it means to create a loving environment for the elderly.

Dear God, I want Dad to be happy and feel secure these days. Help me to gently reassure him.

4. The Great Depression and World War II: Two Common Experiences That Still Influence Seniors

Members of the senior generations share two common experiences that continue to profoundly influence how they think, how they act, and what they see as rock-bottom truth. Keeping each of these in mind will help when you're taking care of your parent.

One was the Great Depression; the other was World War II.

Few families were spared the hardship brought on by the Depression. In some, the breadwinner lost a job. In others, siblings had to be split up because parents couldn't afford to take care of all their children. Children routinely had to drop out of school and take any job they could find to help support their families. Many family homes and farms were lost.

During the Depression and on through the war, Americans learned to make do and do without. They rightfully took pride in their ability to accept those hard times and to live through them.

It's difficult for the generations that have followed to understand the spirit of patriotism and the spirit of sacrifice that swept the United States from 1941 to 1945.

The war touched everyone, from the young men entering military service to those they left behind.

On the home front, women stepped forward to fill the gap in the American work force. Rationing was one way all private citizens were asked to contribute to the war effort.

Members of the senior generation have never forgotten the lessons those events taught them during their childhood and young adult years. On a scale that our country hasn't seen since then, American families learned firsthand what it means to be poor. They learned firsthand what it means to be at war.

As a Depression survivor, your father probably has a strong opinion about money. He knows what happens when — for whatever reason — poverty strikes. This may be why he balks when you try to get help for him.

Mom has always done her part, is proud of her work history and independence, and doesn't want any "handouts" now. Also, she may not understand why today's poor don't "pull themselves up by their bootstraps" as so many did in years past. And she doesn't want to spend a dime unless it's absolutely necessary because a dime is still something precious to her.

The odds are your parent also has a very strong opinion about the United States. In general, seniors have a staunch love for their country and a matching intolerance for those who, in their eyes, are tearing down what they and their peers sacrificed, fought, and died to preserve.

Dad may never have talked to you about what it was like to go to war, much less be in combat. At times he may show intolerance toward the Japanese or Germans. He may have sharp words about any "foreigners" moving into, or having an economic influence on, "his" country.

Your father may feel the younger generations can debate the morality or military necessity of dropping the atomic bomb all they want, but they weren't around then. They can't know what those times were like.

These are some points to keep in mind:

•Mom may refuse to spend money on items or services she really needs for her own health and safety (not to mention basic comfort) because she looks on her savings as her children's inheritance. Providing for the family still comes first.

If this seems to be the case, assure her it's all right for her to spend the money. You *want* her to spend it. She has more than your permission; she has your blessing.

•Dad may say — in all seriousness — he's saving his money for his "old age." It's tempting to laugh but he isn't joking. You need to help him understand it's all right to spend part of that nest egg now.

•Mom may not want a particular service because people "didn't used to need it." She may expect you to take care of her because she took care of Grandma. Remind her that years ago some services (personal home care, for example) may not even have been available and now many people have a need for them because of how society has changed. (Extended families living farther apart, for example, and immediate families with both parents working outside the home.)

•Dad may refuse a government-sponsored service because he won't take "charity." Remind him that for years he put his tax dollars into this system and he's entitled to use it. That's why it's there. He's simply getting a dividend on an investment he's already made.

God, I know prejudice is wrong and can't be ignored. Help me guide Mom to be more accepting of others.

5. Dealing with Your Parent's Racial and Ethnic Prejudices

A newspaper advice columnist made headlines when she referred to Pope John Paul II as a "Polack." It's common for an aging parent to make that same kind of mistake and use a derogatory term to describe someone's race or ethnic background.

Beyond your embarrassment as your parent's adult child and your embarrassment for others around your parent, this kind of behavior can be a slap in the face to the people who are providing care for your mom or dad.

Mom's words aren't necessarily said out of meanness: She's simply reverting to what she learned as a child and to what was commonly accepted behavior during a good many of her adult years. Words that are taboo today freely peppered everyday conversation then.

Dad isn't deliberately trying to offend anyone either, but his prejudices — racism even — stand out more starkly now as society continues to try to move beyond ignorance and hate. His favorite and often-told "jokes" seem even more offensive.

This doesn't mean your parent's behavior should be excused or go unchallenged, but it is important to understand why your parent may sometimes say the things he or she does.

In previous times, segregation wasn't just the norm, it was the law. A person of one race seldom had the opportunity to meet, come to know, or becomes friends with someone from another race. Even different ethnic and religious groups didn't mix as commonly and easily then as they do today. The environment was ideal for stereotypes to flourish. And they did.

Ignoring or glossing over your parent's words or attitudes is made more difficult because it's not uncommon for Mom or Dad's home- or health-care provider to be of another race or ethnic background.

Despite your parent's objections, a home-care agency, nursing home, or hospital cannot legally restrict by race or ethnicity the person assigned to your parent's case. In other words, your parent cannot request his or her worker be of a certain race or ethnic background.

With that in mind, here are some things you can do to help your parent . . . and his or her worker:

•Talk with Dad about the person who is helping him. Emphasize the worker's training and experience. If you're bringing in someone to assist with home care, don't just spring that person on your father and hope for the best.

•If at all possible, stay with Mom and the worker until your parent begins to feel comfortable.

The worker who comes to help her may speak English as a second language and may have a strong accent. It may take your mother a while before she can easily understand what the worker is saying. It will take a lot of patience on both sides.

•After a reasonable trial period, if it becomes painfully obvious Dad isn't going to modify his attitude and choice of words, other arrangements for a home-care worker may have to be made. A worker shouldn't have to face verbal abuse or, as sometimes happens, false accusations.

When dealing with the worker's supervisor, you need to be clear about the situation. It *isn't* that you're dissatisfied with the worker's performance; the fault lies with your parent's attitude. This may be hard to admit, but it would be unfair to offer false or vague reasons for discontinuing services that reflect unfavorably on the worker.

•Don't let your parent off the hook too easily, especially if he or she "slips up" when your children are around. Grandparents can have a profound influence on the youngest generation, teaching bad as well as good.

Remember, none of us is ever too old to learn. None of us is ever too old to become a better — a more loving — person.

Heavenly Father, you gave us life because you love us. Help us always treasure and defend it.

6. Euthanasia and the "Right to Die"

Supporters of the "right to die movement" don't hesitate to admit that physician-assisted suicide would be just the first step toward their long-range goal of making active and even involuntary euthanasia legal in the United States.

As the movement continues to push forward the debate in the political arena with arguments centering on "quality of life" and the "right to choose," society is in danger of further closing its eyes to the value of human life. All human life. Worth is being further confused with productivity, wealth, health, youth, and power.

It's frightening to think your parent might come to believe his or her life means so little that the world — or your family — would be better off without him or her. But that's one of the messages the movement is sending.

And cruelly, the messages are being coupled with the natural human fear of pain. Fear of being in pain; fear of seeing a loved one in pain.

These are some points to keep in mind:

•As Catholics, we believe our life here on earth is not the sum of our existence. While we are merely passing through, the time we spend on earth is precious. A gift from our Creator. There is a time to be born, a time to live, and a time to die. We don't cut life short, but we don't try to prolong it beyond that time to die.

This means, without forcing death or stepping in and hastening death, we let death come. We realize death will come.

• It would be foolish to try to list specific guidelines here for what is acceptable or not acceptable with regard to end of life medical treatment or the withdrawal of that treatment. Advances in science and technology continue to constantly push that envelope. And just because something can be done doesn't necessarily mean it should be done.

Medical ethics are important. Finding out what your parent wants is important. So is talking to a priest or Catholic chaplain about your family's particular concerns and questions.

•Despite what the backers of the right-to-die movement say, pain can be controlled in most cases, and advances continue to be made in the area of pain management. If Dad is in pain, talk to his doctor about it.

•Hospice is a tremendous service. Take advantage of it. *(See chapter 75 on hospice.)*

•The final months, weeks, or days of your parent's life may be very difficult in many ways but they also may be very rewarding. Both for Mom and for you. She may need that time to better prepare to die. To come to terms with death without being afraid. To prepare spiritually. *(See chapters 54-57 on returning to the Church and the sacraments of reconciliation, Holy Communion and the anointing of the sick.)* To make peace with friends or family members.

You may need that time to say good-bye. To prepare to be a survivor, the one left behind.

To miss out on those months, weeks, or days — to cut them short — would be a tragedy.

Elderly Issues

Holy Spirit, please give Dad the wisdom to make the decisions he's facing.

7. Independence, Control, and Self-determination

It shouldn't be a surprise that you and your parent don't always agree on what's best for him or her. No two people agree on everything all the time.

When conflicts arise, what can you do? As you make your decisions, it will be helpful if you keep these three guidelines in mind:

•Encourage and allow independence.

A part of growing to adulthood is accepting, and sometimes demanding, independence. Because of chronic illness or mental deterioration, growing old can mean the chipping away of that personal freedom. A goal for you as a caregiver is to delay or to minimize that erosion. Your role is to offer assistance that helps your parent remain as independent as possible.

This means you don't take over tasks or make decisions Mom can still handle. For example, don't dress her in the morning just because it would take you only five minutes but it takes her twenty. Don't decide she needs a lifestyle that is as active as her health will allow when what she really wants is a quieter schedule because she's lived a long and hectic life and now she wants to rest.

•Whenever possible, let your parent be in control.

It's human nature that we want to be in the driver's seat when it comes to our lives. Giving up control, or having it snatched from us, can make us angry and frightened.

What you see as a mere detail may be monumental to Dad. Maybe he has always gone to the 8:30 Mass on Sunday morning but now you're concerned about his getting there on his own. So you unilaterally decide the two of you will go to the 5:00 Mass on Saturday evening and you can't understand why he's so upset.

After all, you're the one making the sacrifice, aren't you? You're the one doing him a favor.

From your father's point of view, you're trying to ruin his Sunday morning routine. Now he won't be able to say hello to his fellow "8:30 regulars," the friends and peers he enjoys visiting with each week.

Letting him keep some control might mean mutually agreeing that one or two Sundays each month you take him to the 8:30 on Sunday. Let him pick which Sundays. Likely, after a while, he'll feel equally comfortable with "the strangers" at the Saturday Mass, too.

•Remember each of us has a God-given right to self-determination.

We were created to make choices. We were given free will.

This means that in day-to-day living, your parent has the right to determine what his or her life will be like. To do this or to do that.

That's fine in theory, but complicating the issue in the real world of the aging parent and adult-child caregiver is the fact that, sadly, at some point your parent's ability to make safe decisions may begin to fail. Mom or Dad may begin to choose what is dangerous or unhealthy or may lapse into self-neglect.

This is not a valid excuse for you to decide on your own that Mom is "incompetent" and to take over all decision making for her. It's better for you and her to ask a professional — an attorney, for example — to help objectively evaluate the situation.

That person can also help you set up safeguards to protect your parent as much as she needs it at the time. It's possible to design these necessary precautions without losing sight of the importance of her independence, her need to be in control as much as possible, and her right to determine how she wants to live the remainder of her life.

Lord, sometimes it's so hard to accept the losses that are a part of anyone's life. A part of my life. A part of Mom's. The thought of losing her scares me so much.

8. Losses

It helps to keep in mind that it isn't just *how* your parent is feeling; it's *what* he or she is feeling. Quite often, it's a tremendous sense of loss.

In so many areas.

The process of aging is also a process of letting go. Bit by bit. It's losing so many things and being forced to accept the fact that many of them if not most will never be replaced.

True, life is filled with losses. But that doesn't mean we feel a particular loss is the same way at all the different stages of our lives.

Here are three examples:

•A tooth: If I'm five years old and my front tooth starts to wiggle, this is great news! I can hardly wait to show everyone. This proves I'm on my way to getting rid of my baby teeth — and at five, I am *no* baby! — and having "big kid" teeth. It means the tooth fairy will be stopping by some night soon and I'll get money!

If I'm elderly and my tooth begins to wiggle, if it aches, if my gum becomes inflamed. . . . I wonder what it means. Where is it leading? Expensive and painful dental work? Dentures? A change in my diet, to soft, boiled, mushy food? Maybe it would be best just to ignore it. Maybe the pain will go away. There's no need to worry others, not to mention the expense. I'm so tired of trips to the doctor; I don't want to add visits to the dentist.

•A set of keys: If I'm twenty-five and I lose my keys, I mutter and fuss and fume because I might be late for work. Again. Now where could I have put them? I'm *always* losing my keys. It's a minor inconvenience.

If I'm a senior and I misplace my keys, I can't help worrying that I'm exhibiting an early stage of Alzheimer's. Isn't this how it starts with some people? Like my sister-in-law. The one who could never seem to remember where she had parked her car in the mall lot and then, within a couple of years. . . .

•A friend: If I'm forty-five and a close friend moves away, I feel sad. I miss having frequent contact with that person and I suspect, as the years go by, we may drift apart. But I know I can pick up the phone and call him. I can send him a funny birthday card. I can drop him a line at Christmas and keep him up to date on what I've been doing. In the same way, he can stay in touch with me and share his latest adventures.

If I'm old and a good friend dies — and so many seem to be dying so close together these days — it's the end of our friendship. I can remember the good times and I can offer a prayer for his soul, but he is gone. I know there will never be another like him. Perhaps this was a relationship that stretched back to my youth. Someone who really knew me and understood what, together, we had come through. I have lost someone irreplaceable. And it hurts so much.

As any human body ages, there are adjustments that have to be made, limits that have to be admitted. When I am young and strong, I can go mountain climbing. I can scale snowy peaks and look out on fantastic views and feel a tremendous sense of accomplishment. As I get older, I have to limit myself to hiking.

Then walks through the park.

Around the neighborhood.

Until finally, it may be that simply leaving the house takes more energy and effort than I am able to exert.

Step by step, I have told myself, "That's all right. I can still. . . ." But what now? What can I do? If I cannot climb a flight of stairs? If I cannot cross a room by myself? If I cannot get out of bed?

When, in my heart, I still want to be at the top of that mountain.

✳ ✳ ✳ ✳ ✳

As your parent gets older, the physical limitations can be compounded and the problems, the losses, occur more frequently. For example, he or she may experience diminishing or total loss of vision. Of hearing. The inability to control the bladder or bowels or both.

Now your father may think, "Here is my child trying to tactfully explain to me that I should wear . . . diapers! That's what they are. They may have a different name, but that's what they are. Even my grandchildren are old enough that they no longer wear diapers. This is so humiliating."

Or "A hearing aid! I don't need a hearing aid. If young people today would just quit mumbling and speak up."

Or "No, I'm not going to the eye doctor. Every time I go he gives me more bad news and my eyesight is just fine."

It may help you to keep in mind that, as Mom ages and becomes unable to perform the everyday tasks she used to love, she may feel she is losing a part of her identity. Your mother is no longer the "super housekeeper" with a spotless home. Her yard is no longer the prettiest one on the block. She can no longer bring her famous scalloped potatoes to family gatherings.

And if she isn't that great housekeeper, gardener, or cook, what is she? Who is she?

At the same time, with the absolute best of intentions, a grown son or daughter may seem to be taking over. Being downright pushy, is what it feels like to Dad. "You think it's not safe for me to drive anymore! Just who do you think it was that taught *you*!"

"You think I need help writing checks? Why, I was a vice president in one of the largest corporations in. . . ."

"They make me so mad sometimes," a parent may think, "but what if I don't go along with them? Will they put me in a nursing home? Is there some kind of veiled threat here?"

"No!" you may immediately reply, but, again, this has to do with feelings. And feelings can be based on misconceptions.

There are other losses, of course. Among the most difficult is the death of an adult child. That one just doesn't seem right. Children are supposed to outlive their parents.

And probably the biggest loss of all — next to the loss of one's own life — is the death of a spouse.

"This was my best friend, my lover, my confidant, my partner, my support in so many ways for so many years and now that person is gone. Now I need him . . . now I need her . . . more than I ever did before, because I've never felt pain and loneliness like this before.

"It isn't simply that I've lost my spouse. It's that without that person, I'm lost."

God, there's no pain like the pain of grief.
Please bring us comfort.

9. Grief

To grieve after the death of a loved one doesn't mean experiencing a single emotion. Grief involves a host of feelings.

It's commonly accepted that there's a "cycle of grief." There are pieces or periods of the grieving process, but those pieces, those periods, don't necessarily follow a set pattern or stick to a particular time frame. Even after going through one part, the griever may — time and again — return to that aspect of grief. How one grieves, just as how one lives and how one loves, is unique for each individual.

With that in mind, it sometimes helps to understand that within the cycle there are four sections:

•Shock and denial. Mom can't believe this has happened. She hopes perhaps it's all a bad dream. She feels confused. Later, she may not remember some of the things she said or did.

•Anger and guilt. Dad is mad at Mom for dying and leaving him. Mad at God. Mad at the doctor or hospital staff. At the same time he feels guilty. "I should have. . . ." "If only I had. . . ." Then, too, if death followed a chronic illness, he may feel even worse because a part of him may be glad the ordeal is over. He feels guilty because sometimes, in the middle of being a caregiver, he looked forward to the day he could rest.

At this stage in Dad's grief, others around him may seem so stupid. Their concerns so petty.

•Depression. Mom realizes that there's no satisfactory answer to truly explain what has happened. She feels so lonely. She's so tired.

•Adjustment or acceptance. One day, Dad may notice he's getting on with his own life. He's starting to return to his normal activities. But with this comes feelings of disloyalty to Mom. Somehow his moving on is a betrayal.

Elisabeth Kübler-Ross, a pioneer in bereavement ministry and author of *On Death and Dying*, adds one more section. In the middle she includes bargaining. If Mom promises to be very good, no one else she loves will die. If she vows to be perfect, maybe all of this is some kind of mix-up or mistake and Dad isn't really dead.

What can you expect from your parent if he or she is grieving? (Or if you're going through grief?) This is an extremely stressful time. The wide, multi-layered range of emotions shifts constantly.

Your parent's anger, loneliness, sense of loss, and even physical pain can be triggered by any number of things. By realizing "his" favorite television program is about to start. By even thinking about attending Sunday Mass without her. (Many a widow or widower finds it *extremely* difficult to go to "their" Sunday Mass alone.) By seeing an item in the newspaper that would have amused him. By coming up on Christmas, a birthday, an anniversary without her.

By catching a whiff of Old Spice aftershave. By smelling bacon cooking. By holding her hair brush or his hammer. By hearing "their" song played on the radio. By so many things your parent sees or hears or touches or tastes or feels.

In grief's early stages, it's common to feel anxious and vulnerable. To feel ill. There may be a tightness in the chest and throat. Headaches. Fatigue. Stomach problems.

Mom may not be able to eat. She may not be able to sleep or can't seem to do anything but sleep. May not be able to stop crying. May worry that she's going crazy.

Dad may withdraw socially. He may want to be alone, or he may become more dependent on another family member.

What can you do to help your parent if he or she is grieving? (What can you do to help yourself?) These are some points to consider:

•How each person grieves is unique. Mom shouldn't compare how she grieves, or feels the need to grieve, with anyone else's method. The best way for her is whatever works best for her.

•Dad should avoid making any major changes right away. For example, selling the house or moving to another part of the country.

•Mom needs to take care of herself. To eat properly and get enough sleep, even if she doesn't feel like doing either. It may help if, under a doctor's care, she takes medication for a time.

•It may help if Dad "works" on his grief. If, when a feeling surfaces, he doesn't automatically push it aside. To let himself cry when he feels the need to cry, to get angry when he feels mad, and so on.

•This can be an incredibly spiritual time in his or her life. And in yours. Encourage your parent to turn to God.

•Mom may want to consider taking advantage of whatever bereavement ministry her parish or diocese might offer.

•Dad may want to look into taking part in a support group. There are many groups out there, each with a unique character and feel. If one doesn't seem right, he could think about checking out another.

•Your parent may benefit from counseling. A therapist or grief minister can't take away the pain but may help make it more bearable. May help make it easier for your parent to understand why he or she is feeling all those jumbled feelings.

•Encourage Mom, when the time is right, to consider having her own ritual for saying good-bye to Dad. Maybe it's visiting the grave site alone. Maybe writing a letter to him, or doing whatever it is that fits her, that fits them, best.

It shouldn't be a surprise that she feels a need for a private and personal memorial. The relationship the two of them shared was one-of-a-kind, too. It was irreplaceable.

Lord, thank you for the many roles Dad has played in my life. For the many sacrifices he's made for us, his family.

10. When the Parent-Child Roles Reverse

Cook. Chauffeur. All-around fix-it person. Financial officer. Problem solver. Protector. The list goes on and on. Every parent wears a lot of different hats when he or she is raising children and running a household. Some are worn proudly, others grudgingly. No matter how they're worn, everyone in the family knows which hat belongs to each parent. Those are his. Those are hers. Until. . . .

Until everything begins to change as your parent ages and you must start to assume more and more of those responsibilities for Dad or Mom. As you must start to fill the roles that were always his or always hers.

It's not easy to watch these changes happen in your parent. When Dad can no longer drive the car or handle paying the bills. When Mom isn't able to cook or take care of the house.

It's not easy to be a part of those changes. Not for your parent or for you.

It's understandable that an aging parent may have a difficult time giving up those favorite tasks. Maybe Dad is known for his beautiful garden. Mom for her wonderful family dinners. Now someone else will be clipping the hedge or making the pot roast and your parent knows that person can't do the job as well as he or she did. It may seem that other person isn't just doing it differently, that person is doing it wrong!

Your parent may argue, "Just who says I can't do that anymore? You? Why, I was doing that when you were in diapers. Doing it before you were born."

It's no wonder your help is sometimes met with resistance and anger, and is seen as interference rather than assistance.

On the other hand, maybe you don't want to assume so many of those responsibilities but see you must. Maybe you can't have everything just the way Mom did for extended family dinners. Maybe you don't know how to fix Dad's car and so — heaven forbid! — you have to hire someone else to do it. ("A stranger? You're throwing away good money on a stranger to change the oil?")

These are some suggestions:

•If you find yourself and your parent reversing roles, keep in mind that you need to be gentle about the changes that have to be made. Go slowly. Don't suddenly charge in and take control. Start with small things.

•If at all possible, let your parent play a part. For example, maybe Mom can't host Thanksgiving dinner but can still make her famous gravy for it. Maybe Dad has to stay off the ladder but can be the official supervisor when the gutters are cleaned.

•Keep in mind there's another important role that reverses as your parent ages. Growing up, Mom or Dad was the one who chased away the bogeyman, the one who made everything better. Now he or she is scared. Aging — preparing to die — isn't easy.

Now it's up to you to comfort Mom. To reassure her. Not to make everything all right — you both know that can't be done — but to try to make it better than it is right now.

Watching Dad grow old and lose abilities isn't easy either. It's frightening. But now you're supposed to be the one who is strong and brave. Now you can't lean on him because he needs to lean on you.

This is a special time in the relationship between you and your parent. It's a strange and confusing time that brings new challenges as it exposes new facets of the love you share. It's a precious time.

God, help Mom know this is what I really want to do. And then give me the strength to do it.

11. "I Don't Want to Be a Burden"

There are many reasons an aging parent can be so concerned about "being a burden."

One is that, no matter what a family may be saying and doing, our American culture sends a different message. We live in a society that equates productivity with value. One that sees independence and self-worth as synonymous. One that says age means obsolescence.

New is good. Newer is better. Newest is best. Whether it's cars, computers, ideas . . . or people.

A second reason a parent may feel like a burden is the matter of losing control. In the past, Mom took care of herself. (Herself and the whole family!) Now she can't get to the doctor if someone doesn't drive her. She can't walk across the room to get a cup of coffee. She knows she has become so dependent on others.

A third reason for that burden feeling is the issue of pride. It's hard for Dad to maintain his sense of dignity when he can no longer bathe himself. When he needs help getting dressed.

And a fourth reason for a parent's concern is that he or she can see what is happening to you, the adult child. There are times when you're overloaded. Times when stress is running high. Your mom or dad can't suddenly stop being a parent. Can't suddenly stop worrying about you and your health and happiness.

Unfortunately, that can be the time when Mom or Dad raises the subject. His or her "I don't want to be a burden" pops out when you're feeling angry, upset, or frustrated. Typically, the immediate answer is "No, you're not!" Typically, the immediate feeling is guilt.

What can you do? Here are some suggestions:

•Grant yourself the luxury of admitting what you're doing is hard. Remember this situation will not last forever. It's a difficult period, but it's temporary.

•Look for outside support. Try to avoid becoming so overloaded Dad *does* seem like a burden. *(See chapter 63 on exhaustion and care for the caregiver.)*

•Realize Mom may need to be reassured more than once. Yes, you told her that last week but. . . . "What about now . . . or now . . . or now?"

•See if there's some small part of a bigger task your dad can do so that he feels like he's helping out at least a little bit. Or if there's something he can do for you — a token gesture to say "thanks" or to make things easier for you — because of all you've been doing for him. (Setting the table or folding the laundry, for example.)

•Sit down with your parent during a calm time and talk about the idea of him or her being a burden. Let your parent know that providing care is something you want to do. Yes, there are hectic moments, but you see taking care of him or her as a privilege. It's one small — and, at times, not-so-small — way of saying "thank you" for all your parent has done for you.

> *God, please help Dad understand he's relieved of*
> *"active duty" as a parent.*

12. Always a Parent: Worries About Adult Children

Maternal or paternal instinct isn't something that can be shut off — something that simply clicks off — once a child reaches a certain age.

In the midst of all your concerns for your parent, he or she is worried about you. That concern, that love, has been a cornerstone in your relationship. It's not about to suddenly change now.

Your mother can't help but worry when she sees how much her problems, her needs, stretch your patience, your strength, your schedule. She knows you're overworked, frightened, and sad. You can tell her not to worry. Tell her you're fine. But she knows what she sees. She sees the truth.

Unfortunately, she may bring up the subject and insist on dealing with it at a time when you're especially frazzled. *(See chapter 11 on not wanting to be a burden.)*

There are a couple of things you can do to help ease your parent's mind a bit:

•Talk with your parent during a calm time. Let Dad know that if you feel there's some part of caring for him you can't handle, you will get help from someone who can.

•Understand why Mom may suddenly seem like such a busybody. You're around her more than you have been in recent years and so she's more aware of the daily ups and downs you're going through.

Maybe you're upset because your child was sent to the principal's office this morning or the car repair isn't going to be completed for three more days. When you were seeing each other only once every week or two, those might have been ancient history by the time you got together.

When you're down, for whatever reason, she wants to solve the problem or offer possible solutions. Thank her for her concern but let her know you can handle it.

•Let Dad know you're taking care of yourself. Going to a support group if you need it. Having a nice dinner out with your spouse. Asking for help from others. Just as it pleases you when you see that he's taking all his medicine and eating properly, he's happier knowing you're taking good care of yourself, too.

Dear God, give me patience! And stay near.
I'll need more soon.

13. Taking Care of a Crabby or Formerly Abusive Parent

It's hard to be patient when you're taking care of a parent who's crabby. It may not be possible for you to care for one who physically, emotionally, or sexually abused you when you were younger.

Let's look at "crabby" first. It could be Dad has always been grumpy. When you reached adulthood there was a real sense of relief because you could move out and be on your own.

But now he needs your help. He doesn't necessarily want it, and may, in fact, resent it, but he needs it. Each time you approach his front door you feel as if you're entering the lion's den. You hope you'll be lucky enough to come out unscathed.

That's how it is in some cases, but not all. Sometimes a parent who has been pleasant most of his or her life suddenly turns grumpy. This isn't surprising and, most likely, it's temporary.

Mom's change in disposition may be triggered by other things happening to her. It's easy to snap at the people around you, even those you love the most, when you don't feel well. When you hurt. When you aren't getting enough sleep. When you're upset because your independence is quickly slipping away. When you're so frightened about what the future may bring.

But if a change in personality continues to stretch on, you need to talk it over with your parent's doctor. It could be related to a medical, mental, or emotional problem that should be addressed. It could be a side effect of a new medication, one that leaves your mother feeling anxious. Or it could be a prescription Mom has been taking a long time is causing this new and different reaction because her body chemistry is changing.

Whether your parent has been a lifelong crab or is only being nasty temporarily, it's important for you to remember that this is a situation that presents a high risk of abuse. An adult child simply loses control and hauls off and smacks the aging parent.

Obviously, that's never right. Neither is an aging parent hitting an adult child. Sometimes it may be necessary for you to make sure you are at least an arm's length away from Mom or Dad. You have to keep yourself safe.

Here are some suggestions for dealing with a difficult parent:

•Even when the going is rough, keep the basic guidelines for taking care of Mom in mind. She should be respected. She should be treated with dignity.

•During a calm period, sit down with Dad and tell him what he's doing that bothers you. Be specific. It could be your father isn't even aware something is upsetting you.

•Get away completely. Get out of the house, calm down, and try to analyze the situation more objectively. If Mom is pushing your buttons — and nobody can push our buttons like family — maybe you can't stop her but you can control your reaction. By quickly changing the subject. By letting her go on for a time without your arguing and escalating the debate. By realizing it very well could be that no matter how much you do, or how well you do it, she is *never* going to be satisfied.

•Maybe you can't be your Dad's primary caregiver. He simply isn't able to allow that and so fights it — fights you — every step of the way. Look into getting someone else to do the cleaning, the laundry, the personal care and so on.

•Talk with others who understand what you're going through. A support group can be a wonderful release. So can a long lunch with a good friend. You need to remember to take care of yourself, not just for your own sake but for the sake of your parent.

But what if your parent abused you when you were younger?

•You need to take care of yourself. That may mean you simply can't be the one who is taking care of Dad.

•You may need someone to talk to about the emotions churning inside you. Counseling can help. Ignoring memories and feelings — and the many physical, mental, and emotional complications they can trigger and aggravate — doesn't make them go away.

•There's no reason to get down on yourself if you're not able to help Mom. There's no reason to offer an explanation to others who ask "Why?" except to say, "I'm not able to do that."

•It may be you feel comfortable playing the role of the one who arranges for your parent to get help from other people. You do not have to be the front-line caregiver. *(See chapter 49 on hiring a case manager.)*

•It may be clear now that you're never going to be able to resolve this situation with your parent but you may be able to come to terms with it yourself. That may mean you have, at best, a neutral attitude toward Mom. You love her as you would a stranger. You're civil to her, but there is no parent-child relationship or bond there. Your situation is a part of the unfairness that can touch an innocent person's life.

I hate hearing them fight, Jesus. Please give me the strength and wisdom to be a good diplomat.

14. Refereeing Fights Between Mom and Dad

It could be both your parents are still living but one — or both — need your help with caregiving. If that's the case, you may face the added challenge of friction in your parents' relationship.

There are many reasons an aging couple may not be getting along, that their so-called golden years of marriage seem to be anything but that. The sad truth is divorce is common among couples whose children have grown up and moved away.

While a youngster can do little if anything to stop a fight, an adult child may feel an obligation to step forward. To step between. Here are some points to consider if you find yourself in that position:

•Parents are not a single unit. Your mother and father are two individuals who may be at two different points in their lives. Each is dealing with his or her own losses, concerns about what is happening, worries about health, and so on.

•One parent may be becoming more dependent on the other, a development each finds frustrating and frightening.

Maybe Dad was always the strong one. The provider. The caretaker. The guardian. The driver. Now Mom must assume those roles.

Maybe Mom did the cooking, the cleaning, the shopping, the laundry. She balanced the checkbook and sent out the Christmas cards. Now Dad is learning those jobs.

But Mom doesn't drive the same way Dad did. The way he thinks everyone should. Or Dad doesn't cook like Mom always has. The style to which she has become accustomed. This type of role reversal is hard on any two people of any age.

•Maybe Mom and Dad's relationship has always been confrontational. Some couples bicker — take pot shots at one another — throughout their married lives. And each can give as well as he or she gets.

•A personality change could be a symptom of a health problem. Alzheimer's disease, a stroke, or other medical conditions may change Mom or Dad from meek and mild to combative and aggressive. Check with your parent's doctor.

•A woman's role in society has changed. In years past, a woman who was a housewife took care of her children, managed the family home and followed her husband's instructions. Times have changed. An old-fashion husband may have difficulty when his wife tries to change, too.

•Subconsciously, one parent may not want any kind of disagreement for fear his or her last words to a spouse will be words of anger. Instead, Mom or Dad will swallow their words, and the anger will build up inside until one day it explodes over something minor.

What can you do if your parents are having more battles?

First, consider what the fight is about. How important is the issue? Is it a question that needs to be resolved or is it just everyday friction?

Is it something they need to handle themselves? For example, which soap opera to watch while they're eating lunch.

Or is it something big that needs your attention, too? Perhaps Dad wants to move to an apartment and Mom doesn't want to sell the house.

Second, try to avoid taking sides. Talk to each parent separately. Alone. Listen to that person's point of view and try to explain the other's. If the fight seems to be unequal, if one parent really needs help, provide it. For example, it's no longer safe for Mom to drive but Dad can't get her to give up the car keys. Or Mom is in danger of becoming ill herself because taking care of Dad is so taxing and Dad refuses to allow her to spend money on outside help.

And third, remember that the arbitrator's role is always a delicate one, especially when all the parties are in the same family.

Dear Lord, help us remember the good times. Thanks for letting us be together today.

15. Celebrating Birthdays and Anniversaries

Your parent may be approaching a birthday with mixed emotions, a strong combination of joy and sadness.

There can be a wonderful sense of accomplishment: In spite of

all that I have been through, I have survived. I have been richly
blessed.

But there also may be a sense of confusion, anxiety, or even
dread. I never expected to live this long. I didn't plan to. I didn't want
to. Why am I still here when my spouse and so many of my friends
and relatives are gone? How much longer am I going to have to live?
How much more am I going to have to endure? My health was pretty
good on my last birthday, but just look at me now. How much worse
will it be on my next one?

What can you do to help? These are some points to consider:

•Let your parent take the lead. Maybe this is the year Dad would
like the extended family to gather to celebrate his eighty-fifth. Maybe
this is the year Mom wants only a quiet lunch with you and your
siblings.

How do you know? You ask, you talk, and you listen. Most of
all, you listen.

•Rather than feeling festive, an older parent may be feeling
depressed as this emotionally-charged day approaches. When Mom
or Dad mutters, "I wish I had gone. It's time for me to go," it's hard
not to immediately answer, "Don't say that!"

This isn't the time to argue. Just tell your parent why you're
glad he or she is still around. The greatest birthday gift of all might
be to finally say out loud "This is what you mean to me. . . . This is
what you mean to my children. . . ."

•It isn't always easy finding out what Mom or Dad wants for a
birthday present. The first several inquiries may be quickly shot
down. "I want to be younger," or "I want my health back."

In a sense, they're right: Often a good present isn't one that's
bought. It may be one that gives the two of you time together. It's
arranging to go out to lunch once a month over the next year. It's
planning to come over with the kids to fix Mom or Dad's favorite
meal. It's taking your parent to a First Friday or Sunday morning
Mass at the old parish. It's arranging to have a Eucharistic minister
bring Holy Communion to Mom or Dad at home if your parent isn't
able to leave the house.

These are gifts that can mean so much to an aging parent. Gifts that can bring so much comfort to an adult child after Mom or Dad has died. Gifts that can give so many priceless, lifelong memories to grandchildren.

If you're going to have a party for your parent, there a few things to keep in mind:

•Many older people tire easily. Planning a four-hour blowout or open house with dozens of guests might simply be too much.

•These days, with siblings often living in different parts of the country, it might be impossible to get the family together at the same time on the same day. The solution may be several smaller celebrations on different dates. Or maybe a conference call. Or helping your parent place calls, one at a time, to your siblings who can't be there.

Family members can also put together a special "birthday book," either at the party or round-robin fashion if people can't make it to the celebration. Each can jot down a few sentences on a particular topic. For example, "My funniest memory of Dad" or "A lesson Mom taught me that I'll never forget." Or you could arrange a "card shower," contacting relatives and friends and asking them to please send a greeting card to mark the occasion.

•Party or not, sometime on that day, it's good to pause and remember family members and close friends who have died, especially a spouse. All too often the fear of saying the wrong thing or of upsetting a parent prevents an adult child from saying anything. Unfortunately that silence can be interpreted as forgetfulness or even worse, indifference.

That same fear, that tendency to be silent, holds true for noting anniversaries after one partner has died. But it's good to remember as a family. It's good to say things out loud. Maybe Dad just wants a quiet lunch or dinner with you. Maybe Mom would like to attend a daily Mass with you, a Mass being said for Dad. Maybe your parent would really appreciate being taken to the cemetery where his or her spouse is buried.

Keep in mind the best birthday and anniversary celebrations — those that touch the heart — often include tears as well as laughter.

Blessed Mary, I want my children to know and love my parent. Please help me do whatever I can to help make that happen.

16. Grandparenthood

It might never have occurred to you that you are "bi-generational." You are equally at home with your parents or your children.

There really aren't many years that you have both your kids and your folks with you. Not surprisingly, this special time, this blessing, comes with particular responsibilities. As a member of the middle generation, you're being called on to be the bridge between your parents and your children. To be the one who can help them come to know each other better.

These days, this can be hard to do. It's not news that we live in a highly mobile society, and that many grandchildren and grandparents know each other only as visitors or over the phone.

These are some suggestions for helping both generations:

•Teach your children how to show respect for all their elders.

•Remember that your kids are going to pick up and mimic your attitude. If you treat your parent with love, they'll do the same.

•Explain your parent's medical condition or limitations (a restricted diet, hearing loss or confusion, for example) in terms your children will understand.

•Remind your children to speak slowly and clearly when talking with Grandma.

•Let them know just because Grandpa seems grumpy doesn't mean he's mad at them.

•If your parent lives with you, let the children be involved in helping your mother or father in an appropriate way, maybe by vacuuming Grandma's room or reading the newspaper to Grandpa.

•If the generations are a little slow in conversing with one another, if they must rely on the phone, for example, offer suggested topics. "Ask Grandpa to tell you about his first car. It was a Model A." "Mom, Mary would like to tell you about her project for the science fair."

•Perhaps most important, give both generations time together so that they can come to know each other, to love each other as much as you know and love both. Give them time together so your parent can have a glimpse of the future. Give them time together so your children can better appreciate the past and can enjoy the lifelong gift of fond memories of a loving grandparent.

Lord, I really want to hear the story.
I promise to pass it on.

17. Helping Your Parent Write His or Her Memoirs

Most of us tend to think writing one's memoirs is an activity limited to those how have made a fortune, gained fame, or accomplished some remarkable or historic task.

The truth is, everyone has a story to tell. Each person — an individual created and loved by God — has led a unique life. An older person who takes the time to write down some of those experiences, to share some of those memories and those lessons, gives a tremendous gift not only to children, grandchildren, and even great-grandchildren, but benefits himself or herself as well.

Your parent may have, with wisdom and with age, become more reflective. It's common for an older person to feel a need to review his or her life. While many may consider jotting down some of the highlights, most quickly dismiss the idea because they don't want to appear pretentious, and others aren't really sure how to begin.

Here are some suggestions to share with your parent:

•Begin by beginning.

The hardest part is getting started, but Dad *doesn't* have to start at the beginning of his life. He can begin by writing a little about something, some time or someone that was important to him.

He can start with one or two of the basic philosophies he's tried to follow or found to be true. For example, "Treat others the way you want to be treated." Or with pieces of advice he would like to pass along. "You get what your pay for."

He doesn't need to get hung up on writing "My Autobiography." Instead, suggest he jots down a few memories of his father or mother. The home where he was raised. The day he met his spouse-to-be. His grandparents. After all, he may be the last family member who knew them and can tell stories no one else can.

•Don't be intimidated by grammar, punctuation, or spelling.

This is an exercise done for love, not for an "A." You and your mom can always go back, proofread, and make corrections, and if she makes mistakes, who cares? Ask her to imagine reading a letter written by her great-great-grandfather describing his life. Would she treasure it less, put it aside, or lower her opinion of him because he had misspelled a word or failed to put a comma in the right place?

•Choose the method and style that best suit you.

If Dad likes to type, then let him type. If he prefers a pen and pad of paper, he should use those. If he feels more comfortable writing a paragraph or two each on a variety of topics, he can do that. If he wants to use a tight outline form, that's fine, too. He can write a book, a collection of short stories, a handful of letters, a journal, or choose whatever other form works best for him.

Your father doesn't need to be concerned about keeping it all in order as he's writing. He can go back later and take care of that, if he still wants to.

•The more you write the more you will remember.

One story, one memory, quickly leads to another and soon there are many things to write about. Going through old family albums can spark many memories. Family members will appreciate having a record of who previously owned heirlooms — a ring, a pocket watch, a dish, or bowl — that have been handed down from earlier generations. Dad could write a little bit about each piece.

•You can go high tech.

If your parent prefers talking to writing, he or she can use a tape recorder or video camera. Sometimes it helps to have an "interviewer" — you — present. You can ask Mom some questions.

This can be a very special time for both of you, precious time spent together.

Also, it may help to have some of the old family albums on hand. As the two of you go through them, she can reminisce about the family and friends pictured.

If Mom's worried about gaps of uncomfortable silence on the tape, play some period music softly in the background. She can show her grandkids that today's music can't compete with the Big Band sound she enjoyed so much.

•What you're creating is priceless.

Dad's "life review" may help him take pride in the fact that through good times and bad, he has survived. Then too, after Dad is gone, his words will bring consolation, encouragement, and happiness to his descendants.

Dad may discover that there are areas, there are relationships with other people, that need to be resolved. Reminiscing can lead to the opportunity to forgive or to ask forgiveness.

In the end, a parent's memoirs often come down to simply recording how he or she was loved and how he or she returned and passed along that love. It's focusing on what really matters, on what life is really all about.

Living Arrangements

Dear God, I can't be with Dad every minute.
Please protect him.

18. Home Safety

You may be used to "disposables" — everything from cameras to contact lenses — but you need to remember that members of the senior generation, those who lived through the Depression and World War II, were taught from their earliest days to make do with what was on hand. To use it up. To wear it out. *(See chapter 4 on common experiences.)*

Unfortunately, that means in the homes of some elderly people, they're "making do" with a hodgepodge octopus of ancient extension cords rather than having a wall outlet fixed or buying one cord of the proper length and correct electrical rating.

They're "using up" old prescriptions, even though the doctor has taken them off the medication.

They're "wearing out" items like toasters or space heaters or fans to the point that there's a danger of shock or fire.

They're emphasizing self-sacrifice and thrift to such an extent that their safety is jeopardized, and that can be a serious, even deadly, mistake.

In the same way that a couple expecting their first child have to baby-proof their home for safety, you need to walk through your parent's house with safety in mind.

First, are the basics covered? Some items need attending in any home. For example, no overloaded electric outlets. Sufficient smoke detectors. A bath mat in the bathtub. No exit doors blocked by furniture. No drapes, furniture, or other flammable items near electric baseboard heaters. And so on. *(For information on a more complete check list, see "Resources" in the back of the book.)*

These are just a few suggestions:

•Remember all stairs, inside and out, need sturdy handrails and they need to be well lit.

•Make sure the bathroom has a grab bar. Don't use an empty towel rack for this. Grab bars are designed — and installed — to bear the weight of an adult. Called "adaptive equipment," medical supply stores offer literally dozens of similar safety items — from bath tub rails to raised toilet seats — that can make a home safer. Many stores also rent items and have catalogs available.

•See to it the kitchen has a sturdy step stool — or none at all. Also, move bulky and heavy items to lower cupboards because it may be difficult for your parent to reach up and lift things down. Items taken from lower cupboards, even if dropped, will land directly on the floor, not on Mom or Dad.

•Put a night light in Mom's bedroom or make sure she can easily reach a lamp from her bed.

•Get rid of clutter. Furniture buried in mounds of junk mail and floors stacked with old newspapers and magazines can make it difficult for anyone to get around and especially someone using a cane or walker.

•Help Dad throw out prescribed medication that he no longer needs or has passed its expiration date. Some seniors just *hate* to throw away a "perfectly good," passed-date prescription just because it cost so much. You can remind him that outdated medicine loses its effectiveness, and older medicine, combined with his current prescriptions and conditions, could cause serious side effects.

•Make sure medicine bottles are clearly labeled in print large enough for Mom to read. (The same applies for household cleaners.) If she has trouble remembering what medicine to take when, use a seven-day medication dispenser (available at drug stores).

•List needed phone numbers, in large print that can be read without glasses, by each telephone. These should include your work and home numbers, the doctor's office and the general emergency 9-1-1. Also, program those numbers into any speed-dial systems. And write down your parent's address. When a crisis arises, anyone can forget his or her own address.

•Remind Dad to be safety-conscious. For instance, don't smoke in bed or just before nap time in that favorite chair. Don't wear the bathrobe with the floppy sleeves when cooking something on the stove. Don't use the stairs for storage.

Most of your suggestions won't be new to your parent. Mom may seem a little annoyed as she answers, "I know, I know." Don't let that discourage you. It's probably the same answer you gave her years ago when she was first teaching you these valuable lessons.

Two other points to consider:

It may be worthwhile to see about an emergency response system for Mom or Dad. Using a necklace and/or a "panic button," your parent can simply push a button and the system automatically telephones for help.

Ask your parent's doctor about companies offering the service. Find out if the response is local or if it's monitored in another part of the country. And if it is called, do staff operators then call you or call the police in your parent's area?

Also, be aware that some of the companies in this fairly new industry emphasize sales (they're vigorously pushing entire home-alarm systems), but fall short when it comes to service.

Another choice is a reassurance phone call. Again, ask your parent's doctor about this. With this system — often administrated by the local hospital — someone calls your parent at the same time every day to make sure he or she is all right. If there's no answer, the person informs whoever is on your parent's needs-to-be-contacted list.

*Heavenly Father, winters in the North can be cruel and
brutal. Please keep Mom warm and safe.*

19. When a Winter Storm Leaves Your Parent Homebound

When the weather outside is frightful, it's especially important
for you to have a plan in place that will ensure your parent stays safe,
warm, and well fed.

A winter storm can quickly down power lines and restrict
travel, leaving Mom or Dad in a dark, cold house or apartment with
no help in sight. Here are some points to consider to help both of you
be better prepared for this kind of emergency:

•Even the most independent person may feel more than a little
uncomfortable when bad weather means that, for days on end, it will
be impossible for him or her to get out or for anyone else to get in. A
simple daily telephone call can work wonders in providing that
needed reassurance.

Also, be sure a list of important numbers (family, friends,
neighbors, doctor, parish, and community resources) is posted by your
parent's phone.

•Arrange for help *before* the snow hits. If it's going to be
impossible to travel from your part of town to your parent's, or if you
live an even greater distance from your parent, arrange to have a
neighbor, a member of the parish, or a volunteer do some grocery
shopping for Mom. Even if she doesn't need anything from the store,
ask that person to stop in and make sure your mother is doing all
right.

•As anyone who has ever lifted a half dozen shovelfuls of wet
snow knows, removing the white stuff from a sidewalk puts a
tremendous strain on the heart. It's not something an aging parent
should attempt. Set up ahead of time for a kid in the neighborhood to
shovel your dad's sidewalk and take care of any ice. Be sure to let the
worker know you'll pick up the tab.

•Encourage Mom to stay indoors. Even if she's bundled up and
walking only a short way, ice and snow often lead to falls and broken

bones. It's better to suffer a little cabin fever for a few days than spend weeks or months laid up in bed.

•Have emergency supplies ready at Dad's place in case the power goes out. Make sure they're stored in a place that is easily accessible. This would include a flashlight with fresh batteries, transistor radio, non-electric clock, nutritious food that doesn't need to be cooked, and a manual can opener.

•Remind Mom that food in the refrigerator and freezer may keep for several days if the doors aren't opened frequently or for any long period of time.

•If Dad is taking medication, be sure there is enough on hand to last through any snowbound days. Remember that even though he might not be able to get out, others probably can, and many pharmacies make home deliveries for a slight fee.

•If Mom is on some type of life-support system, such as oxygen, contact her doctor and the local electric company ahead of time to see what they recommend. (You may have to provide a small backup generator.)

•Your father will stay warmer in a home or apartment without heat by wearing layers of clothing (underwear, pants, light shirt, heavy shirt, sweater, jacket, heavy coat, hat, gloves) rather than one bulky winter coat.

•If the fireplace is to be used, be sure the chimney is clean and the screen is in place. Remind Mom not to try to heat a room with a barbecue, a hibachi, or any other type of grill which emits carbon monoxide.

•If the furnace has gone out but the electricity is still on, make sure Mom or Dad:

Does not try to heat with an appliance, such as an oven, with the door wide open.

Does not overload an electrical outlet or extension cord with an electric heater.

Does not have *anything* near an electric space heater.

Does not use candles for heating or for light.

•Remind your parent it's all right to call 9-1-1 if he or she isn't able to stay warm or fix meals and no one else is available to help.

•Remember, if you lose contact with your parent, you too can call 9-1-1 and ask a police or community service officer to do a welfare check on Mom or Dad. Better still, you can ask that your parent be placed on a check list of people in the community to be contacted if a storm strikes. Sometimes officials want to know who might need help in an emergency so assistance can be planned.

Lord, help me be gentle but firm, protective but respectful.

20. Helping Your Parent Give Up the Car Keys

We are a nation of drivers. We define ourselves by the automobiles we choose. I'm wealthy; I can afford the latest luxury sedan. I'm thrifty; I tool around in a subcompact that gets great gas mileage. I'm adventurous; I go everywhere in a pickup truck with a camper. And on and on.

In the United States, getting one's driver's license is more than obtaining the state's permission to operate a motor vehicle. Every sixteen-year-old knows it's a rite a passage. A giant step on the road to adulthood. A key to independence. A time to celebrate.

In the same way, losing one's driver's license, losing access to one's own car, is more than forfeiting the state's or the family's permission to drive. Every elderly driver knows that this too, is a rite of passage. It's seen as a giant step on the road to one's final days. A tremendous loss of independence. A time to mourn. *(See chapter 7 on independence and chapter 8 on losses.)*

It isn't easy on families when the day comes that an adult child must tell an aging parent that it's no longer safe for him or her to drive. It's a sad time for both.

In many families — perhaps most — it was a parent who taught the children, one by one, how to drive. A child felt safe with Mom or Dad at the wheel. But the aging process — the gradual and, in most cases, inevitable deterioration in vision, hearing, and reaction time — changes that.

If an older person has some general confusion, a minor irritant in everyday home life can be dangerous or even fatal when it comes to driving.

Again and again, you must ask: Is this safe? Is it safe for my parent to keep driving? Is he in danger of harming himself and also of harming others?

It's the lucky family that has an older parent who realizes and can admit the physical limitations that have occurred, who understands the danger to himself or herself and others, who voluntarily says, "I can no longer drive."

Unfortunately, sometimes those who have become least capable, those at the highest risk, are the ones who not only refuse to admit any problems but refuse to even discuss the possibility with a concerned adult child. And self-imposed restrictions ("I don't go out on the freeway," "I don't go down that busy street," "I don't go out at night") offer only a false sense of security.

These are some suggestions if you're concerned about your parent's driving:

•Talk early and talk often with Mom about your concerns with her driving. Let her know that when she is no longer able to drive, you will be available to help her get around or to arrange rides.

•Don't swoop in one day and confiscate the car keys. This almost guarantees anger, resentment ,and a nearly total lack of cooperation.

•Prepare what you're going to say. Stick to the facts. (Accidents, close calls, rising insurance rates, failing eyesight, and so on.) Don't get caught up in your parent's anger and begin firing back.

•Enlist the help of your parent's doctor to explain why this action is necessary.

•If Dad has given you power of attorney, refer to that when discussing this issue, as a reminder that he trust your judgment. If someone else has power of attorney, ask that person to help you with the discussion.

•Don't expect much help from the department of motor

vehicles. In general, they tend to be generous when it comes to letting drivers with questionable ability keep their licenses.

•Perhaps most important of all, keep in mind that you cannot take away the car keys without actually providing some backup. You need to help your parent figure out how he or she is going to get around now. When can you drive? When can your siblings? When can your spouse or children? What about neighbors or friends? Are taxis or buses possibilities? Call the local Senior Information and Assistance number to find out about special low-cost van rides for the elderly. *(See chapter 47 on finding help and "Resources" in the back of the book.)*

•And finally, know that your love, respect, and concern can ease your parent's sense of loss, but can't eliminate it.

Holy Spirit, sometimes I'm not sure what to do. Help us find the best place for my mother.

21. Nursing Homes and Other Options

Black or white. One or the other. At home alone or in a nursing home. Unfortunately, some families think those are their only choices when it comes to deciding where an aging parent can live.

The truth is these are simply the two extremes on a broad spectrum of choices. Within that range are a host of options that can be examined and evaluated.

Where to begin? The first step is to ask your parent what he or she would like.

Does Mom want to stay in the family home? Would Dad prefer to move to an apartment?

Sometimes a parent feels that the cost and energy needed to keep up the house is just getting to be too much. It would be a relief to no longer have that responsibility, but there is the fear that the next and only step is a nursing home.

If your parent wants to stay put but needs more help, a number of services are available in most communities. If it's simply a matter of Mom getting out more often and being with others in the least restrictive setting, a senior center may be the answer. Or if she needs to be watched more closely, an adult day care center.

If in-home help is needed, in addition to visiting nurses there are visiting physical therapists, occupational therapists, and other health-care professionals.

Home care such as shopping, laundry, cooking, cleaning, and the like as well as personal care such as bathing can also be arranged. Many seniors are able to stay in their own homes with only a minimum of assistance, perhaps as few as four or five hours a week. Or you may need someone to be with your parent during the night. This type of help is available in many communities.

Another option is a home-sharing program that matches elders who remain in their own homes with others who are looking for a place to live. In some cases the tenant pays rent. In others, a barter system is set up. For instance, the tenant takes care of the shopping and cooking and is always there during the night.

Or maybe the best choice for your parent is an adult family home. Licensed by the state, these provide a family setting for the elderly person and assistance with particular needs such as bathing or monitoring and taking medication.

There are also retirement communities designed for and restricted to seniors. These may offer planned social activities but not services. The community may be private condominiums, apartments, or mobile homes.

A retirement home, on the other hand, often has a range of services and costs — from a private apartment with limited services such as meals and housekeeping to assisted living and on to complete skilled nursing care.

Your parent might enter at one level and, as necessary, accept more and more help. And pay more and more money.

If the retirement home is a "rental residence," there is no entry fee but the tenant pays a monthly amount, which can be steep. At a "life care residence," the tenant actually buys into the place with a large sum and then pays a monthly fee. At some retirement homes, the up-front money is thousands of dollars.

Prices, methods of payments, and services vary. Don't be afraid to ask questions when visiting any of these facilities. Be sure to find out if any of the expenses will be covered by Medicare or Medicaid.

And don't be afraid to raise this topic with an aging parent who is still living at home and doing well. Helping Mom or Dad investigate what options are available in the community before he or she need help can go a long way toward alleviating anxiety and misconceptions.

Holy Spirit, I need to be a good observer and a wise planner. Help me be both.

22. Choosing a Nursing Home

In a perfect world, your parent would never have to go to a nursing home. In a near-perfect world, both of you would have already explored nursing-home options and made decisions before the need arises. In the real world, you may be doing the investigating and choosing alone as Mom or Dad is about to be discharged from the hospital.

Here are some suggestions for making that choice less difficult when visiting nursing homes:

•Take a sibling or friend along to help you more clearly evaluated the home.

•Don't be shy when asking about costs. A nursing home admissions director may quote a figure, but you need to find out what is included, what costs extra, and what that additional costs will be. (In some, even disposable bed pads or diapers are considered extras.)

Ask what's covered by Medicare, Medicaid, private insurance, and private pay. Ask if your parent's bed will be held if he or she is temporarily hospitalized.

•Ask how a patient's care plan is written. Is it personalized or does a general plan apply to almost everyone? Find out who monitors the care plan. Ask what happens to that plan if your parent's health improves or gets worse. Can you be involved in the planning?

•Ask if one doctor is assigned to the nursing home, if there are several doctors, or if a patient may continue to use his or her own physician.

•Walk through the facility. Look around inside and out. Is it clean and well maintained? Are the halls stacked with various equipment because there isn't enough storage space? Is there a smell of urine?

Look at the patients. Do they appear well-taken-care-of? Are they clean and shaved and is their hair combed?

Look at the rehabilitation unit. Most nursing homes have a room for physical and occupational therapy. Is the equipment falling apart? Is it being used at all?

Check out the activity calendar or bulletin board. What's planned? Is it busy work at a preschool level or are there projects and programs that would really appeal to seniors and contribute to their mental and physical health? Walk around the activity room while it's being used. Are the people enjoying themselves? How many are taking part? Talk to the residents.

A good plan is to walk through, talk to the admissions director, and then walk through again, about an hour later. You should be able to tell if there has been some activity. Are all of the patients still in the same place? No patient should be in a hallway "waiting for lunch" for an hour.

Many places will be happy to let you have a meal at the home. Ask to be served whatever the residents are being served. Is it nutritious? Does it look and taste appetizing?

•Ask about security. Not just protecting the patients from someone wandering in, but protecting them from stealing by fellow patients. This is not uncommon. Find out who is responsible for monitoring this, to whom one reports a problem, and what the procedure is when something is missing.

•Ask how room assignments are made. Obviously rooms will be

all-male or all-female, but are matches done according to compatibility or is it just the next person through the door gets the next vacant bed? What's the procedure if problems arise between roommates?

•Find out if there's a continuum of service. If your parent's health gets better or worse, will he or she need to move?

•Ask who helps with the transition when Mom or Dad first moves in. Depression is typical and certainly understandable.

•Get a copy of the nursing home's "bill of rights" for its clients.

•**Don't sign a contract during that first visit**. Go home and think about it. Take notes during your visits to several homes so you can remember what you saw and where you saw it.

•Once your parent is in a nursing home, get to know the staff and make sure they know you. The more contact you have with them, the better care your parent will receive.

Holy Spirit, what's best for all of us?
We need your guidance.

23. Should Mom or Dad Move In?

Sometimes honesty hurts, but in the long run, it may cause the least amount of pain for you and your parent if you're seriously considering having Mom or Dad move in with you.

Any discussion about this new living arrangement needs to begin with two key questions. First: Have other possibilities been considered? And second: Is this something *both* generations want?

If you're considering having your mother or father move into your family home, remember that adjusting to such an arrangement takes a commitment by your parent, by you, and by your family. Often the emotions each felt before the move — worry, stress, guilt, anger, jealousy and so on — aren't eliminated by the new arrangement; unfortunately, they're intensified.

Sometimes the move just isn't right, for a variety of reasons. It's nobody's fault that Dad is a late riser and you have a houseful of young children who are up at the crack of dawn every day.

It's nobody's fault that your house is already too small and simply can't accommodate one more person.

It's nobody's fault that you were recently promoted at work and right now your new duties leave you little time for anything else.

It's nobody's fault that you and your parent get along better with a little more space — physical and emotional — between you, and that living under the same roof will bring up old issues and attitudes toward one another that neither wants.

It's better for both of you to be honest from the beginning. The hurt from hearing "this won't work" is less painful than the hurt of living in a situation that could possibly tear the family apart.

You need to ask yourself: Why do I want to do this? Is it because I *have* to? Is it because I'll feel guilty if I don't? Is it because my parent or siblings or other family members are in some way forcing me to do it?

Or do *I* want to do this? Is it an opportunity for my children to get to know my parent better? Is it a chance for me, in some way, to give something back to my mother or father? Is it an opportunity for both of us to spend time together, time that is passing so quickly?

When the daily grind begins to take its toll — and having anyone of any age move into a household can stir things up — you need to have that basic reason to fall back on.

Yes, today you're tired but. . . . Yes, today was a hard day but. . . . Yes, tempers flared today but. . . . You know why you agreed to do this. You know why this is good not just for your parent but for you.

OK, God, we've made the decision. Now help us make this work for everyone.

24. When Mom or Dad Moves In

Having your parent come live with you may be the right move, but that doesn't mean it will be easy for either generation. Being aware of each others feelings and concerns can help make the transition a smooth one. Here are some points to consider:

•The move is stressful for both your parent and you because it's a time charged with emotions.

Your father is grieving not just because he has lost his family home or own apartment, but because he has lost his way of life. He may have had to say good-bye to his friends, neighborhood, and parish.

Then too, the change has more than chipped away at his sense of independence and control. He doesn't have a home anymore. He must accept the fact he's living in his son's or daughter's home.

You may be grieving also. It's hard to watch a parent's health deteriorate. It's hard to see the family home — the home of your childhood — up for sale. It's hard to give up some of your privacy, and ask your spouse and children to do the same, by having someone new move in with you.

The result may be that both of you — parent and adult child — feel as if you must tiptoe around the other person, holding in any emotion that might be considered negative. But if this new arrangement is going to work, then, like all strong and healthy relationships, it must be based on a loving and respectful honesty and openness. On a two-way street of communication willing to accept and give helpful criticism as well as praise. Keep in mind:

•Your parent needs to be given as much control as possible.

Things that may be trivial to you may be important to your mother. Ask if she would like to move in at the beginning of the month or the fifteenth. Let her decide how to decorate her room. What color would she like it painted? What material and pattern for the curtains? What furniture and other household items would she like to bring with her?

Reducing a houseful of belongings collected over a lifetime to fit into a single room will be a very difficult task. Be respectful as you help her sort out the items. Old newspapers, trinkets, and bric-a-brac may be priceless to her. Treat every item as if it were a treasure.

Let your parent decide what she will take with her to your house, what she will toss, what she will give to charity, what she will give to family members.

Keep in mind that Mom may want to distribute a good deal of her possessions while she is still alive. She's not being morbid; she just wants to enjoy seeing each person inherit his or her special gift.

•Maybe your parent would like to be given some household duties.

Dad may feel less like a burden and more like a contributing member of the family if he takes his turn drying the dishes or one evening a week oversees a homework session. Maybe sometimes he can watch the kids while you and your spouse go out to dinner. (But he's not a built-in baby-sitter.)

•Your parent needs more than food and shelter; your parent needs your emotional support.

Even if Mom was strong and optimistic when she lived on her own, the dramatic change in her life and the host of emotions that come with that change can easily lead to depression. You need to be available. You need to realize there is also a time commitment on your part with this arrangement.

Having your parent move into your family home can be a tremendous blessing if each member remembers a home is more than just a house, a family is more than just a group of people living together.

Each member is entitled to a loving and caring environment. That's the goal facing all of you: How — together — you can make that happen.

Thanks, God, for the memories.

25. Saying Good-bye to the Family Home

Many, if not most, families at some point find themselves saying good-bye to the family home. It's a special time in the life of a family. A unique moment. A forced period of reflection as family members remember what has been. What, in some ways, will be no more.

There will be no more sharing Thanksgiving meals in that dining room with the two older generations elbow-to-elbow at the table (with all the leaves taken from their special storage place and carefully inserted to make it maximum size). The younger generation giggling at the little kids' table (siblings and cousins so glad they don't have to eat with those boring adults).

There will be no more placing the Christmas tree (a big one this year when Mom gets to pick it, a small one next year when it's Dad's turn) in that corner. Right there. The best spot. Tried and true.

No more glancing down on a crisp spring morning and noticing that the first shoots of tulips have popped through the dark earth in the flower garden by the front walk.

No more sitting on the patio on a hot summer afternoon with hamburgers or hot dogs hissing on the barbecue grill.

No more watching each autumn as the leaves change from green to gold on that little tree in the side yard. (Well, quite a big tree now. Dad planted it what year?)

Over the years a family home fills with hundreds, if not thousands, of items; it is crammed with even more memories.

There are the good times: birthdays, anniversaries, holidays. And the hard times: illnesses, periods of unemployment, deaths.

Sometimes the move is bittersweet. Mom is leaving — and it's difficult — but she's moving into a lovely smaller home or apartment. She's bought a condominium. She's going to a retirement community that better suits her needs now. She's heading for a warmer climate.

Sometimes sorrow dominates the move. Because of age or illness, Dad isn't able to take care of the house anymore. Taxes, insurance, and maintenance on the house take too big a bite from a fixed income. The neighborhood has changed; it's no longer safe. Mom has passed away and Dad really isn't able to live alone.

For the widow or widower, saying good-bye to the family home can feel like, once again, having to say good-bye to that loving spouse. This was their house. Their home. From the time they first saw it on the market until long after the mortgage was burned, they were partners here. Raising a family. Growing closer to one another. And now, alone, it's time to leave.

If your family is getting ready to say good-bye to the family home, here are a few points to keep in mind:

•Remember, Mom gets to decide what to keep and what to give away. Junk to you may have a lot of sentimental value to her.

Dad may need your help sorting and packing; moving takes a lot of work and there's always a lot of worry. (And you may finally have to do something with those boxes of your stuff you've been storing in his basement or attic.)

•Take some pictures of the inside and the outside of the house. Of course the family has taken hundreds of snapshots there for years and years, but maybe not of each bedroom. The family room. The basement. This house is part of your family's history.

Better still, walk around with a video camera. Let the family join you for a running commentary. "Here's where we kept track of how tall each child was." "This is the window that was broken twice in the same week by the same baseball." "Dad built this bedroom onto the back of the house after Susan was born."

•Come together for one last meal to say good-bye. Sometimes families make it a final Thanksgiving, Christmas, or Easter. Or they gather for a parent's birthday. It's an opportunity to share memories; to laugh and to cry.

•Don't forget that a house is only a structure. Some walls, a floor, and a roof. It's the people and the love they've shared that have made this building so special. Those people, that love, aren't being left behind, they're simply moving to a new address.

Remember, the home didn't make the family; the family made the home. The family is still there.

Physical Health

Dear God, please help all physicians use their knowledge and skills with compassion.

26. The Doctor

It's easier for everyone concerned if your parent has a primary doctor he or she trusts. You don't necessarily need a physician who specializes in geriatric care, but you do want one that's comfortable working with the elderly.

It's better, too, for the doctor-patient relationship to be established before your parent needs to hear bad news. Dad is going to be much more likely to believe what he's being told, and do what his doctor asks him to do, if he already has faith in his physician.

These are points to consider in choosing and visiting a doctor:

•How do you find the right doctor for your parent? Ask Mom. Would she prefer someone younger or older? Male or female?

And ask the doctor. From what hospital does she work? Does she accept Medicare patients? Does she accept the health insurance your parent has?

•Tell Dad not to worry about hurting his doctor's feelings by going to a different one — even if he's been seeing the first physician for years. Loyalty is a noble virtue but the first concern here is getting your father to the best doctor for him now.

•Don't be surprised if Mom is very anxious about seeing her doctor and that her anxiety builds as the appointment gets closer. Once there, she may want to be done with the visit as quickly as possible and may be too brief in describing her problems or concerns and too quick to nod that she understands what the doctor is saying when, in fact, she doesn't.

•Under the current managed-care system, physicians often don't have much time to spend with a patient. You can do a couple of things to help. First, ask Dad's permission to go in with him. Before the visit, jot down the questions and concerns both of you have so you'll remember them. And take notes during the visit, too.

Second, if you know there are a lot of issues you're going to need to discuss or if Dad felt too rushed during the last visit, ask for extra time when setting up the appointment. Many doctors are willing to set aside "double appointments" when requested.

•If you have serious concerns about Mom, you can set up an appointment to see her doctor alone. This is much more respectful than having her in the room and then talking about her as if she isn't there. Also, it may be easier for you to talk about her confusion, her incontinence, and so on without her being there.

Her doctor can't give you information without her permission, but you're free to give him an update.

•Encourage Dad to be honest with his doctor. To state the facts without minimizing problems or concerns.

•Also, encourage him to tell the doctor what he prefers concerning end-of-life issues. For example, maybe, if at all possible, he wants to avoid going into a nursing home. On the other hand, maybe because he's so concerned about overburdening his children, he sees a nursing home as a good choice and wants to find out more about it.

•Remember, by being an advocate for your mother, you're helping her doctor do a better job of providing care for her. You're helping her not to "fall through the cracks" in a system which, at times, can seem very impersonal and bloated with bureaucracy.

Remember, too, if your parent isn't getting good care, you can demand it. And if that quality care still isn't provided, you both can choose a new doctor.

*Heavenly Father, help us find the answers and understand
what's happening.*

27. Getting a Second Medical Opinion

It's good for adult children and their aging parents to remember
there's nothing wrong with getting a second medical opinion.
Sometimes it's exactly the right thing to do.

If a doctor has given your mother or father a diagnosis that just
doesn't seem possible — or just doesn't feel right for whatever
reason — to your parent or to you, getting that second opinion is
important.

A second examination may prove the first diagnosis was wrong
and a different treatment is needed. Then again, it may confirm what
the first doctor said and make it easier for your parent and you to
accept the hard truth you're hearing.

With that in mind, here are some points to consider:

•Your mom (or you) may hesitate to ask for a second opinion for
fear of offending the doctor. Maybe he or she is someone the family
has been going to for years. Don't let that stop you. Any good
physician has no problem with a patient seeing someone else to get a
second opinion.

A good doctor knows that sometimes a patient won't believe the
diagnosis without hearing it more than once. Also, a good doctor
always wants to be a better doctor. This kind of physician wants you
to get the best care possible and also wants to know if he or she has
misdiagnosed a problem.

•It could be Dad is the opposite of the one who believes a
doctor's words are carved in stone, the one who thinks it would be
sacrilegious to seek a second opinion. Maybe he doesn't believe any
doctor unless the physician says the words he wants to hear. If he
wants a third, fourth, or fifth opinion simply to finally get the "right"
diagnosis, it's a waste of time, energy, and money. Reassure him it's
time to stop.

•Ask your mother (or yourself) why she thinks a second opinion
is necessary. Don't discount a vague "something just doesn't feel

right about it." Maybe Mom thinks the doctor didn't really listen to what she was explaining. Maybe the doctor was very abrupt in presenting a diagnosis. Maybe the diagnosis just seems too pat and doesn't reflect all the symptoms Mom has. Maybe her condition is getting worse despite treatment for a particular problem.

•If the concern centers on the doctor listening and taking the time to explain, set up another appointment with him or her. Make this one in the office, not in the examination room. Go with your mom or dad and explain what's going on and what concerns you and your parent have. Ask the doctor what determined the diagnosis he or she gave.

•Get information on the disease or condition that has been diagnosed. Many (such as cancer, heart disease, stroke, and diabetes) have national organizations and local chapters. Contact them for up-to-date, accurate information. A national organization can sometimes suggest local physicians who specialize in treating that particular disease or condition. *(See chapter 47 on finding help and "Resources" in the back of the book.)*

•Sometimes a disease or condition has a wide variety of symptoms. Even though your parent and a neighbor have the same problem, they may have very different symptoms. Sometimes books at the library are out of date and the information presented in popular magazines is incomplete.

•Some doctors do better with older patients. Mom or Dad may feel more comfortable with a geriatric doctor, one who chooses to specialize in working with the elderly. The bottom line is that your parent needs a doctor he or she can trust.

Holy Spirit, I feel caught in the middle. Please help me remember you're with me always.

28. When the Professionals and Your Parent Disagree

There's the rock and there's the hard place. There's your parent and there are the professionals. One is saying — begging for — this; the others are strongly recommending that.

And there you are. Wanting to make Mom or Dad happy. Wanting to make sure your parent is safe and well cared for. Wanting to be anywhere but between those two opposing forces.

Mom doesn't want to move to a nursing home. Dad doesn't believe he needs someone in the house twenty-four hours a day if he's going to remain there. She is absolutely set against surgery. He would be crushed if he had to give up his driver's license. But that's what the doctor is saying. The visiting nurse. The social worker.

What can you do?

It helps to realize the first and natural reaction is: "This can't be true." No child wants to hear the bad news that a parent's condition is deteriorating.

It's easy to find excuses. "Mom has always been forgetful." "Dad never had good eyesight." "She was just tired." "He got confused with all those questions."

It's tempting, too, to look at this professional, this outsider, as someone who is merely trying to drum up business. Like an unscrupulous auto mechanic or a shady door-to-door salesman.

Maybe more than anything else, it simply hurts to hear that news. It hurts to have someone say a parent's health is getting worse. It hurts to be so bluntly reminded of a parent's mortality.

Remember, a professional assessment is based on a range of abilities covering a number of areas: physical, mental, emotional and social. Everyone has strengths and weaknesses within that range. An assessment is not a test where seventy percent is passing and sixty-nine percent is failing.

A health care professional has the responsibility, the training, and the experience to see the overall picture, to assess a person's general well-being. To recognize whether or not an older person is receiving the proper care, or if that person is safe under his or her present living conditions.

Also, you need to keep in mind that a professional looks at many, many seniors where often the family comes in contact with only a few older people.

If your family has questions about the accuracy of that assessment, by all means, get a second opinion. If the concern is a "salesman only going after more business," know that Senior Information and Assistance *(See chapter 47 on finding help and "Resources" in the back of the book)* can provide the names and numbers of independent professional assessors who are not associated with any nursing home, clinic, or other senior service.

Obviously, the news you don't want to hear can be even more devastating for your parent. It can immediately bring so many questions, so many fears.

One way you can show you *are* on Mom or Dad's side is to help answer those questions, help address those fears. Together, you can get more information. You can explore what the realistic options are. You can join a support group that welcomes both an aging person and his or her family members.

It's important to remember that the danger in giving in to the temptation to blame — and ignore — the messenger is that the message is also lost. Very often, it's a message that can enhance the quality of your parent's remaining time on earth, and that is what every concerned caregiver wants.

*Thank you, Father, for the many people who have
dedicated their lives to the medical care of others.*

29. At the Hospital

The sights, the sounds, the smells . . . a hospital seems like a different world to most of us who aren't in the medical field. It's a foreign place where we don't know the language, the rules, the customs. So when your father or mother must enter one, often it's not just a time of worry and fear, it's also a time of confusion, both for your parent and for you.

These are some suggestions for making the experience easier:

•Keep in mind you're entitled to ask questions. If your parent has OK'd it with his or her doctor, it's perfectly all right for you to call your parent's physician, identify yourself, and find out what's happening now and what's being planned. In most cases, a physician will be very willing to discuss your parent's condition with you.

•If Mom is being seen by more than one doctor, begin with the primary doctor and ask him or her for the names and telephone numbers of the specialists who also are treating her.

•Once your father has been admitted to the hospital, introduce yourself to the staff on the floor to which he has been assigned. (This can be done over the phone if you don't live near your parent.) Find out what a typical daily schedule is for that floor. This way you'll know the best time to call or visit.

•Ask when your mother's doctor makes rounds. Usually this is done early in the morning and again in the evening. These are the best times to see her doctor and ask questions. The doctor may have a great deal of important information to share, so much so that a patient of any age may feel overwhelmed. It helps to have two people hearing that information, to have two people who can ask questions.

•If you or your parent think of questions ahead of time, jot them down so you'll remember to ask. And jot down the doctor's answers, too. Sometimes it seems as if there are so many health-care professionals seeing Mom or Dad that it's hard to remember who's who and who said what. Make a note of those things as well.

•Ask what social services are available, including information about a visiting chaplain or Eucharistic minister. Find out if the hospital has a chapel.

The social services department is also where you would contact the discharge planner. This is usually a medical social worker who coordinates the discharge of patients. He or she looks at what is happening now — receiving information from doctors, nurses, occupational and physical therapists, and others — and what will happen when your parent goes back home or on to a nursing home or assisted-living facility.

The discharge planner is the one who lines up visiting nurses and therapists and has referral information about non-medical assistance such as housekeeping. Patients are discharged sooner now than they were in the past and may come home while still needing catheters, wheelchairs, and so on. The discharge planner is the person who can arrange for the physical or occupational therapist to teach you about the devices your parent may need.

He or she is also the one who lines up equipment for home use, often through Medicare. Don't be shy about asking for items for your parent; red tape and regulations can make it much more difficult and expensive to obtain that same equipment after your parent is back home.

•Meet with the discharge planner *early*, before you receive word your parent is going to be discharged. Often a patient is given less than twenty-four-hours notice and, while it's going to be great to have Mom or Dad back home again, this may not be enough time get everything lined up to make sure that homecoming is a safe and successful one.

Dear Lord, I never want to forget Dad's sweet smile or his wonderful laugh.

30. The Dentist

In another of life's little ironies, you may find yourself being the one who reminds your parent to brush and floss daily. You may be the one who arranges for those annual or better yet, semiannual trips to the dentist.

Whether it's a parent talking to a young child or an adult child talking to an aging parent, the rules of good oral hygiene remain a basic part of good health. With that in mind, here are some points to consider:

•While it's tempting to believe "if it ain't broke, don't fix it," another maxim is more accurate when it comes to your parent's teeth: "An ounce of prevention is worth a pound of cure."

•A person who lives alone is less likely to cook nutritious meals. It's easier to snack instead. Sucking on hard candy or sipping sugary soft drinks promotes cavities whether you're eight or eighty.

•It may be that your parent hasn't been to a dentist in a long, long time. It may help to remind him or her that methods and equipment have improved a great deal since the '50s and '60s.

•Remember that, as with physicians, some dentists are better with older patients. Look for one your parent feels comfortable with and trusts. Ask around. Check referral services to find out who works with the elderly.

•When there are options for the type of treatment your parent needs, help Mom or Dad in the decision making but *don't* step in and make it yourself.

•Anyone of any age may go to great lengths to hide a tooth or gum problem. Be on the lookout for warning signs: a change in eating habits (a switch to soft foods or an almost liquid diet), a change in chewing (obviously using only one side of the mouth or having difficulty tearing food with the front teeth), swelling in the jaw, reddening or bleeding of the gums, and foul breath.

•It shouldn't be surprising that a mouth changes as years go by.

The greatest dental danger for a youngster is tooth decay. For an older person, it's gum disease, which causes up to seventy percent of all tooth loss. Periodontal disease doesn't affect just the gums. It can also impact the bones and tissues that help hold teeth in place.

•If your parent needs full or partial dentures, pay particular attention to the dentist's instructions regarding their use and maintenance. It takes time to adjust to new teeth. Be aware your parent may resist using them. *(See chapter 8 on losses.)*

•Don't try to fix partials or dentures yourself. Repair kits are available but they may lead to sores as well as irritate the tongue, gums and cheeks. If your parent's dentures become loose, it may be because of a change in his or her gums or jawbone. Let a dentist check it out.

•Tell your parent's dentist if the family has a history of oral cancer. Its warning signs include white or velvety red patches that can't be rubbed away, persistent sores or swelling, repeated bleeding, and a place of numbness or pain. Oral cancer is very treatable in its early stages.

Lord, when my schedule gets especially hectic, help me see what's important and what's not.

31. Vision

Most of us, as the years go by, experience a gradual decline in our ability to see. Getting reading glasses or changing to bifocals is almost a middle-age rite of passage. With an aging parent, a major vision loss maybe due to illness, not just getting older.

If Dad's eyesight is failing badly, it's critical that he has the problem checked by a physician. The same holds true if the family has a history of diabetes. If that's the case, he should have his eyes examined more frequently.

Mom may have what's known as "low vision." This means any combination of glasses, contact lenses, surgery, and treatment aren't going to keep her eyesight within the normal range. If that's the case, the goal for both of you is to help her use her remaining eyesight to its full potential.

Among the common complaints your parent may have are:

•Presbyopia (pres-bee-OH-pia). This is trouble focusing on fine print.

•Floaters. These little wisps are normal and usually aren't a symptom of a medical problem. However, if there are also flashes, this is a reason for concern. Having floaters *and* flashers isn't within the normal range.

•Dry eyes. This is when the tear ducts don't make enough fluid to keep the eyes wet.

•Excessive tears. With this condition, eyes are especially sensitive to wind, light, and temperature.

Other illnesses or conditions that may affect your parent's vision are: cataracts, the transparent lens of the eye becoming cloudy; glaucoma, too much fluid in the eyes which puts excessive pressure on them; diabetic retinopathy, blood vessels not delivering enough blood to the retinas; and a variety of retinal disorders, including retinal detachment in which the inner and outer layer of the retina separate.

Even without suffering from an illness or low vision, your parent may not see as well as he or she did when younger. It's common that there is less peripheral vision, that it takes longer for eyes to adjust from light to dark, that colors fade and depth perception isn't as distinct. (All of which makes driving especially hazardous.)

How will you know? Maybe Mom has stopped doing her needlepoint or reading for pleasure. Maybe Dad is tripping over things. Maybe she looks more disheveled because she can't see the stains on her blouse or wrinkles in her dress. Maybe he has food in his refrigerator past the "don't use" date or isn't following the directions printed on his medication.

These are things you can do to help your parent:

•Keep in mind that Mom may feel especially vulnerable if her eyesight is failing. She may isolate herself, and she probably is very frightened at the thought of "going blind."

•Make sure Dad's house or apartment is well lit. Put in higher-wattage light bulbs (still within the safe and recommended range for the lamp or fixture, of course). Have multiple light sources from different directions. A single bright light makes dark shadows.

•Light the top and the bottom of staircases.

•Mark the edges of any steps with a *contrasting* color, not just a light or dark one.

•Make sure Mom has a night light. Leave the bathroom light or hall light on. Have a lamp within reach of the bed so that she can turn on the light before getting up.

•Arrange the furniture in a pattern that makes it easy to get around. Get rid of clutter, and once your parent is familiar with the furniture's pattern, don't rearrange it.

•If Dad is still driving, encourage him to stop.

•If Mom's place is going to be repainted, use contrasting colors to help her distinguish between doors and walls.

•Have important information such as emergency phone numbers and addresses written in large, thick print.

•Get a telephone with an oversized key pad.

• Invest in a good magnifying glass.

•See about large-print books and magazines and talking books.

•If you live a distance from each other, call rather than write. Or send each other taped rather than written letters.

•Remember your parent has a problem seeing. Be ready with the everyday support that can make such a difference. Offer Mom your arm as the two of you come to a curb. Read Dad the menu if the restaurant is dimly lit or the print is too small. Help your parent keep sight of the fact that it's the two of you together who are facing this challenge.

*Heavenly Father, be with us when I have to tell Mom
things she doesn't want to hear.*

32. Hearing Loss

While hearing loss is not limited to older adults, this is the
common misconception. And because it is, your parent may hesitate
to admit to the problem. After all, admitting hearing loss would be an
admission to being old.

Then again, Mom may not realize she has a problem. If you live
nearby and see her often, you may not notice for a while either. That's
because often there is a slow, gradual decline in the ability to hear well.

Mom may naturally compensate by trying to see your face as
you talk to her. She may turn the television volume up higher than
she did only a few years ago. Frequently, she may ask you to repeat
what you've just said.

The change may be more obvious, more dramatic, if you don't
see your parent for a year or two. Then it may be apparent Dad just
doesn't seem to be catching a good deal of what's being said.

As hearing loss gets worse, your parent may hesitate to carry on
a conversation for fear of answering inappropriately, and actually
may be guessing some of the time about what's being said. Chatting
with another person, or especially a group of people, can be hard
work, and so Dad may visit with others less often. Go out less often.
Stay home alone more often.

If you suspect your parent has a hearing loss, have him or her
evaluated. Usually, the evaluation is done by an audiologist who
checks for sound as well as speech (this type of testing is more
accurate than a simple beep-test in a doctor's office).

If it's determined your parent does have a hearing loss, consider
the following:

•If a hearing aid is recommended, shop around. The price can
range from several hundred to several thousand dollars. As in many
instances, the cheapest may not be the best deal and the most
expensive may not be worth the additional cost.

•Be sure the hearing aid ear piece fits. Think of the fitting as the midpoint in this experience. Remember, it will take time for your parent to become emotionally and physically used to using a hearing aid.

•Don't expect Mom or Dad's use of a hearing aid to be the equivalent of his or her having glasses. Not only is there still a social stigma against hearing aids, but a hearing aid doesn't compensate for poor hearing as well as glasses do poor vision. While the technology for hearing aids continues to make amazing advances, it still hasn't matched what glasses do for failing eyesight.

Whether your parent needs a hearing aid or has such a slight loss that a device isn't necessary, there are things you can do to make hearing loss easier for him or her:

•Avoid shouting. This distorts your speech and makes you sound angry. Speak slowly and distinctly.

•Try to keep conversations face to face. Don't call from another room and expect to be heard. Don't turn away or cover your mouth when speaking.

•Get Mom or Dad's attention first then say what's important. Start with a "leader": "I was just thinking . . . it might be time to start fixing dinner." "Dad . . . have you taken your medicine today?" This gives your parent time to focus and concentrate on what's being said.

•When you want to visit, cut down on background noise, things like the washer, dryer, dishwasher, television, fans, and so on. Also, it will be easier for your parent to hear the television if other background noises are eliminated.

*Thank you, Lord, for a parent who always made sure there
was healthy food on the table when I was growing up.
Now it's my turn to do the same.*

33. Nutrition

There are many reasons helping an aging parent develop and
maintain a healthy, well-balanced diet may be a challenge for an
adult child.

As the body ages, the digestive system is more prone to
heartburn and to constipation. Dental problems may make chewing
painful. Some medications suppress a person's appetite or promote
weight gain.

Depression can bring on a change in appetite. Dad simply may
not care about food. If there is memory loss, Mom may forget to eat
or may think she has eaten. Finances may be tight. Some older
people, after paying for rent and utilities, have little left over for
buying food.

It can be difficult to eat alone. To cook for one person. It's so
much easier to skip a meal or nibble on less nutritious food when no
one else is there.

And then, too, we each develop our eating habits over a
lifetime. While we may know about the basic food groups or the food-
guide pyramid, knowing and following are two separate things.
Changing lifelong habits is very difficult.

As the adult child of an aging parent, you can encourage your
mother or father to eat well. This doesn't mean being pushy or
disrespectful. It doesn't mean ignoring a parent's wishes. In fact, the
more your mom or dad is involved in the process, the more likely it is
to succeed.

•A first step may be to talk to your parent's doctor and ask for
the help of a nutritionist, someone who can tell you what your parent
specifically needs. Sometimes this will include your parent keeping a
daily journal of exactly what he or she eats. (The results can be
surprising for your parent, but then we would probably all be
surprised if we kept track of what we really ate each day.)

•Encourage your parent to follow his or her recommended diet. For example, one that is low-salt, low-sugar, or low-fat; one high in fiber; or one with an emphasis on calcium. When the family gets together, be sure foods on the diet are included in the menu — and don't serve your parent food he or she isn't supposed to have.

•Also, check with the doctor to find out if any of your parent's medications would react negatively to particular foods (to milk, for example).

•Be careful with vitamin pills. They aren't the catchall that makes up for poor eating habits. It's possible to take too many vitamins. And they're expensive.

•Keep in mind that some older people find it easier on their systems to eat six smaller meals during the day rather than three regular-size ones.

•Make food preparation as easy as possible for your parent. Small portions may be frozen and then taken out and heated in the microwave. Make sure the food looks appealing.

•Check out local community resources to see what kind of meal delivery program is available. Maybe your parent would like to go to a nutrition site at the local senior center.

•Remember, no one likes to eat the same foods day after day. Encourage a variety within the boundaries of the prescribed diet and be sure to include the items he or she prefers.

•When grocery shopping for an aging parent, realize it's easy to fall into the trap of buying only ice cream or cookies or some other single food because "that's all she wants" or "that's all he'll eat." Like all of us, your parent would prefer to live on a single, favorite treat; like all of us, he or she needs nutritious food for good health.

Holy Spirit, give me courage. Alcoholism is such a wicked disease and it's so very hard working with — or sometimes even being around — someone who has it and still drinks.

34. Alcoholism

Alcoholism in a family is a touchy subject no matter the age of the alcoholic. Denial, one of the most basic symptoms of the disease, may be used by both family members and the alcoholic.

To make matters worse, among many older people, alcoholism still carries the strong stigma that this is simply a moral weakness and in no way a physical illness. In fact, an older person may be more susceptible to the effects of this disease for several reasons.

The first is age. An older body has greater difficulty processing alcohol. Maybe Dad has only been a social drinker, but as he advances in years, the same amount packs more of a wallop and its effects last longer because his tolerance level has dropped.

The second factor is medication. Many older people are taking a variety of medications that shouldn't be combined with alcohol. When Mom drinks a glass of wine or two with dinner, it mixes with the drugs already in her system.

The third reason is that an older person may want the numbing that comes from drinking too much. While alcohol seems to dull both physical and emotional pain, it eventually compounds both.

And the fourth reason an older person may be more susceptible to alcohol is that society has a better net for catching the younger alcoholic. The police stop him for drunk driving. The boss notices her productivity is down at work. A husband or wife spots a spouse's problem and courageously speaks up.

An elderly person may not be driving anymore, is probably retired, and may be a widow or widower. This means that the older person doesn't have to get up the next morning and face an employer. The widow doesn't have anyone else in the house or apartment to raise a question or an eyebrow as, day by day, the bottle is brought out earlier and earlier.

The temptation, the great temptation, for adult children is to ignore the situation. to rationalize mentioning it. It's bound to cause a fight and maybe you're simply overreacting. After all, Dad doesn't have that much time left. Shouldn't his final years or months be happy ones? Drinking seems to be his only pleasure.

Experts on alcoholism answer those concerns this way: First, if you suspect a problem, there probably is one. It will only get worse. And second, your parent is *not* happy. An alcoholic who is drinking is not a happy person. Those final years or months will not be happy for your parent if the drinking continues. But that's not to say quitting, at any age, is easy.

Also, continued drinking may in fact be shortening Mom's life. It's chipping away at her health and increasing the risk of accidents.

You need to keep an eye out for any warning signs of alcohol abuse: mood swings; general confusion; becoming more isolated; bruises from bumping into furniture or falling; burns from falling asleep with a lit cigarette; a lot of empty bottles leaving the house; and "nesting," making one spot, usually a comfortable lounge chair, an entire world with cigarettes, ashtray, TV remote, glass, and bottle within reach.

As a caregiver, your task is especially difficult because mood swings, confusion and isolation can be caused by many things. You need to seek professional help and — this is important — you need to tell the doctor, nurse, or social worker about your concerns about alcoholism. All too often, if the family member doesn't raise the issue, alcoholism remains buried.

Al-Anon is there to help your family. Alcoholics Anonymous, especially groups for older people, may help your parent.

A good preliminary step is to call Senior Information and Assistance *(See chapter 47 on finding help and "Resources" in the back of the book)* and ask about a geriatric evaluation on alcoholism. At this point in your relationship, there may not be a better way to show how much you love your parent.

*Dear Lord, help my family deal with this powerful
addiction and with the harm it can cause.*

35. Tobacco

The arguments for why a person should quit smoking are many.
We've all heard them. We all know them. They're printed on every
pack of cigarettes sold in America.

Smoking increases one's risk of asthma, heart disease, chronic
bronchitis, emphysema, general pulmonary disease, ulcers, strokes,
and cancer.

Secondhand smoking means that those around the smoker —
spouse, children, grandchildren — are exposed to a host of chemicals
and carcinogens.

Smoking is exorbitantly expensive, taking not only money from
the family budget but healthy years from the smoker's life. When one
smokes, years of parenthood and grandparenthood — like an old
cigarette butt — are simply snuffed out.

Certainly the easiest way to quit is never to start in the first
place. But years ago, when members of the senior generation began
puffing away, smoking was considered glamorous and sophisticated.
And the medical facts available now weren't known then.

Your parent may say he or she is too old to quit. The habit is too
ingrained. But it's never too late. And at the moment your parent
stops smoking — even if he or she has had a lifelong habit — his or
her body begins to heal.

There are thousands of good reasons why a person should quit
smoking. In the end, it doesn't matter *why* your parent stops smoking.
It only matter that he or she does.

It's important that you understand what's involved in smoking.
And what happens to a body when it stops getting that nicotine.

These are some points to keep in mind:

•Twenty minutes after a smoker finishes a cigarette there is a
craving, a need, for another nicotine hit. This intense feeling passes if
the person doesn't light up another one. But if he or she does, twenty

minutes after finishing *that* one. . . . That's the problem, the hook, with having "just one more."

•This isn't just a chemical dependency but a lifestyle habit, too. It may be almost impossible for your mom or dad to imagine morning without that cup of coffee and a cigarette. Or that cigarette after a good meal. Or watching television. Or reading the newspaper. Smoking just goes with so many things, and doing those things without smoking doesn't seem right. Doing them without smoking is very hard.

•The first few days after quitting are the worst. Physical withdrawal is complete by week three. Overcoming the lifestyle habit can take longer.

•It doesn't matter what method your parent uses to quit. The important thing is to quit. Maybe Dad can do it "cold turkey." Maybe Mom needs a doctor's help. Maybe he or she has to join a stop-smoking group.

•Free written material on quitting smoking in available from the American Cancer Society. *(See References in back of the book.)*

•Your parent needs to have an emergency plan for when he or she really, really wants to smoke. Maybe Dad will walk out on the front porch. Maybe Mom will read an anti-smoking pamphlet. Dad will get up and circle the dining room table five times. Mom will go wash her hands and face. Your parent needs to just do *something*!

•Some people need to keep their hands and their mouths busy. They chew gum or suck on candy or fiddle with sunflower seeds. They destroy paper clips or fold paper airplanes.

•Dad shouldn't leave his smoking paraphernalia lying around. The favorite ashtray. The trusty lighter. The rack of pipes. They seem like old friends. They're not! If he can't give them away or throw them away, he needs to at least put them away.

•Help Mom make a list of why she wants to quit. Encourage her to review, and add to the list, often.

•Plan a reward for your parent. Maybe Dad can buy himself something nice with the money he's saving by not spending it on tobacco. Maybe Mom wants to splurge. A tour-bus day trip for the two of you.

•At least for a while, Dad should avoid friends who smoke. They can exert tremendous peer pressure. In fact, quitting smoking may cost him a friendship or two for a time. Mom needs to be around nonsmokers and ex-smokers. (Her fellow nonsmokers and ex-smokers.) They will welcome and encourage her. Every ex-smoker knows how hard it is to quit. Every ex-smoker knows it's worth it.

•Dad needs to drink a lot of water. His body is flushing out its systems.

•Mom should keep some low-cal snacks on hand. If she's on a restricted diet, this means snacks that are all right for her to eat.

•Encourage your parent to pray about this. And you pray for Mom or Dad, too. Pray that your parent will have strength and endurance and patience (and that you will, too). Pray that he or she can succeed, because the battle your parent is waging isn't an easy one but it's one that's so very important.

Heavenly Father, Dad was there when I needed someone to help me learn to walk. Help me be there for him now.

36. Problems with Mobility

We crawl and then we walk. We walk and then we run. We go from here to there without even thinking about it. Mobility is more than a symbol of freedom; it is an act of freedom. But while mobility helps give our lives independence, it doesn't always last a lifetime.

Obviously, the best way for your parent to stay mobile is to simply keep moving. The adage "use it or lose it" remains true. It's so much harder to go through, to endure, physical therapy and make a comeback than it is to remain in relatively good shape to begin with.

When an accident or disease chips away at a parent's mobility or takes a sudden swipe, it's hard on both generations. A parent may be forced to admit he or she is getting old and there will be an end. A child can no longer deny what's happening to a mother or father.

An arthritic hip. A neurologically impaired foot. A leg, or two legs, that must be amputated because of complications brought on by diabetes. An entire side that is frozen by a stroke. There are so many ways an aging parent's mobility — freedom, independence — can be hobbled. When this happens, what can you do to help Mom or Dad? Here are some points to consider:

•Remember what an emotional time this is for your father. He may deny any help is needed. May "forget" a cane or walker. May refuse to use a device in public. May be frightened, discouraged, and angry. Who wouldn't be? Coming face to face with a brace, a cane, a walker, crutches, or a wheelchair is hard.

•Don't fight with your parent! Keep in mind that in this situation, as in so many, you may find yourself performing a balancing act. You dance along that tightrope between taking over completely or saying nothing even when Mom is doing something that seems foolish to you. Finding the proper balance is never easy, and it varies not only from family to family but from episode to episode.

You need to encourage and you need to support, but you are not helping if you step in and do it all. Let Mom complete the task, even if it takes her longer.

•Admit it's hard to see someone you love struggle. Remember that many times it's the only way that person will gain new skills and new confidence. The only way he or she will begin to regain some independence.

•Solicit the support of outsiders — doctors and physical therapists, for example — to deliver the same message you're giving.

•Make sure your parent has the right equipment and it's properly fitted. Make sure Mom or Dad understands how to use it; understands the correct posture, the correct stance, the correct rhythm and speed. An occupational or physical therapist can make this easier. Make sure your parent understands why the equipment is necessary.

•Take the training yourself. That way you'll know, when the two of you come to a curb, which leg goes where and where the cane needs to be. You'll know how to get a wheelchair down a ramp. You'll know how to help Mom or Dad get into and out of a car.

•Give your parent time to adjust. Picking up the skills needed to use that device can't be learned in an afternoon. Mom or Dad may need time to practice at home before stepping out into the world.

•Remember that if your parent is beginning to recuperate after a loss in mobility, things may never be the way they were before, but they can be much, much better than they are right now.

Some days Mom seems so fragile, Lord, but I know you're with her. Thank you.

37. Wheelchairs, Walkers, and Canes

A wheelchair, walker, or cane may seem a mixed blessing. On one hand, it offers security. On the other, it's a constant reminder of a disability.

Whether your parent needs to use a wheelchair, walker, or cane temporarily following surgery or an accident, or has to depend on one permanently, there are things you can do to help make that transition easier for both your mom or dad and for you.

•Get the piece of equipment that best suits Mom's need. These days the variety is incredible, from very basic to extremely complex. A cane may have a four-footed base, a walker may have small wheels at the ends of two of it legs, and wheelchairs can be powered and adjusted electrically. Find out from your mother's doctor or physical therapist what will work best for her. And ask her which style she prefers.

•Don't let cost make the decision for you. As we've written in other chapters, the most expensive may not be what's right for your parent. The cheapest may not get the job done.

See what equipment your parent's insurance will pay for. Check out what Medicare covers. Find out about renting equipment or getting it on-loan from the hospital. Renting or borrowing makes a lot of sense if the device is going to be used only temporarily while your parent regains the ability to walk unassisted.

•No matter the source of the equipment, make sure it fits. Canes, walkers, and wheelchairs have to be the right size to offer the correct support a patient needs. The doctor or physical therapist can tell you if a particular device needs to be adjusted or if it simply can't be used in your parent's case.

•Keep in mind both you and your parent need to learn how to properly use the equipment. *(See chapter 36 on mobility.)*

•Before Mom or Dad returns home with the new wheelchair, walker ,or cane, make sure the house is ready. This might be as complicated as building a ramp or as simple as replacing a carpet with one that's easier to walk on. It might be necessary to move or remove some furniture to make more space for maneuvering.

•If you're helping your parent in a wheelchair, tell him or her what you're going to do before you do it. "I'm going to turn you around so . . . ." "I have to tip back the chair to . . . ."

•Remember, it's going to take time for your parent to get used to this new method of getting around. There's a sadness, a sense of loss, that comes with the realization that a wheelchair, walker, or cane is needed. And it can be frustrating. What used to be done so easily, without even thinking, now — for a time at least — takes hard work and concentration.

God, I want to always treat Dad with compassion and respect. Help him keep his dignity and his pride.

38. Incontinence

The prime-time television advertising is there because the market for the product is there and manufacturers know it. The commercials feature a girl-next-door movie actress well known to the senior generation, and she's talking frankly about adult diapers. Even so, the subject of incontinence remains taboo in many families, and often a senior believes he or she is the only one who suffers with this difficult condition.

Incontinence — a lack of control over the bladder or bowels or both — is more common than the general population realizes. No matter what form it takes, from a mild dripping to the total inability to control the bladder and the bowels, incontinence may be extremely embarrassing for your parent.

We're all taught from an early age that only very small children have accidents. The major step of going from diapers to "big girl" or "big boy" underpants is met with applause from siblings, parents, and grandparents. The reverse step of returning to diapers seventy or eighty years later is met with silence. A parent doesn't want to admit the need, and a family doesn't want to discuss it.

These are some points to keep in mind:

•Your father may begin to isolate himself, staying at home because it seems too risky to venture out. Too risky to go to Sunday Mass. Too risky to take a bus. Too risky to enter someone else's home.

Even if your mother doesn't say there's a problem, you should watch for signs that something is wrong. Maybe she's remaining at home all the time now and her excuses just don't make sense. Maybe she no longer lets you help her with her laundry or allows you to change her bedding. If both parents are alive, maybe Mom and Dad have moved to separate beds. Maybe there's an odor in the house that wasn't there in the past, an odor to which the person with incontinence has become so accustomed he or she no longer notices.

•Dealing with the issue is not easy but it needs to be done. The most critical step is making sure your parent is seen by a doctor. The reason could be a serious, physiological condition or something as relatively minor as a bladder infection. There could be a medicinal reason — a change in a parent's medication or the dosage of a medication that is causing or could stop the problem.

Some theories suggest that incontinence is diet-related or brought on by allergies.

•There may be a solution. There may not. In either case, while Dad is dealing with incontinence, he needs to watch how much liquid he drinks late in the day. It's also a good idea to make sure the path to the bathroom is clear or to keep a commode near the bed. Washable upholstery coverings can help.

When there is an accident, take care that his embarrassment is kept to a minimum. That his needs aren't met with finger-pointing, snide remarks, or hurtful jokes, but with efficiency and respectful, compassionate care.

Mental Health

Dear Lord, it's so hard to watch as Mom slips away. Even when she can no longer recognize me, help her recognize my love for her.

39. Dementia and Alzheimer's Disease

It's become common to incorrectly use "Alzheimer's" as a catchall for describing all kinds of dementia.

The word "dementia" means memory loss and the loss of thinking and reasoning ability. Under that broad term are number of subcategories:

- Alzheimer's;
- multi-infarct dementia, which is stroke-related;
- and other forms, including senile dementia and alcohol-related dementia.

Historically, all types of dementia were called "senility." An older person "became senile."

Certainly your parent has heard of, and known, people who, as they have aged, have "lost their minds" (to use another common expression). Even if Mom is seriously incapacitated because of physical problems, she may proudly and thankfully state, "At least I still have my mind."

Small wonder that Alzheimer's concerns her. The disease has become well known and it — or any form of dementia — takes a horrible toll.

These are some points to consider:

- What complicates this issue is that some memory loss is common among the elderly. What's not normal, what needs particular attention, is severe memory loss.

But what does "severe" mean? If Dad's memory loss impairs his daily activities, if it significantly affects his independence, it can be called severe.

•In the case of dementia following a large stroke, the changes may be obvious and sudden. With other forms of dementia like Alzheimer's or brain cells being damaged by a series of small strokes, the changes may be difficult to notice because they're so gradual.

•Beyond memory loss, dementia may include judgment impairment. There may be personality changes. Mom was so prim and proper but now four-letter words are part of her speech. Dad was always gung ho but now he just sits quietly. More difficult still, a parent may act out sexually, disrobing at inappropriate times, for example. Also, there may be aphasia, the inability to come up with the right word at the right time.

•If the decline is gradual, in its early stages your parent may be aware of it and be very frightened. Dad knows something is wrong. He may feel frustration, depression, and anger and want to isolate himself.

•If you suspect Mom may have problem, it's important she sees a doctor. If there are other reasons she's suffering from memory loss, it may be possible to stop and reverse what's happening. (Dementia, on the other hand, can't be stopped or reversed.) The cause could be a new medication, a combination of the medication she's taking or a change in her metabolism that's altered the side effects of a medication she's taken for some time. Depression also mimics dementia.

•Don't be satisfied with a five-minute medical "assessment" of Alzheimer's. Ask for additional testing. Ask for a second opinion. Ask for a psychiatric work-up. Ask if there's a nearby university medical center conducting dementia assessments.

And if your parent is diagnosed with dementia, these are some suggestions for you:

•Get support for yourself. Become educated. The road ahead will not be easy but it may be less frightening or surprising if others are there to help you. If you know what, typically, dementia can include. Remember, dementia doesn't follow a set pattern or time schedule. And having gone through a particular stage doesn't mean your parent won't return to that problem or show those symptoms again.

•In the early stages, you can help Dad with his remembering by writing notes, setting up a calendar, leaving messages, and so on.

•As the condition progresses, keep in mind Mom can't control what she's doing. She may need to be constantly pacing. To repeat the same question over and over. Obviously, it doesn't do any good to say "I just answered that." Instead, keep your response short and simple and then try to help her move on to another subject.

•Realize Dad may exhibit what's known as "confabulation." He may make things up to fit the circumstances. If he's lost his wallet "someone broke in the house last night and stole it." If he's been standing on the wrong corner waiting for a bus that never came, "the bus company changed the route and didn't tell anyone."

•Try to accept the fact Mom may not remember all that you've been doing for her lately. And, in fact, she may tell others just the opposite — that you've neglected her. It can help to look at your parent's dementia the same way you would view any physical illness.

If she had a stroke and was no longer able to get out of bed, you wouldn't hold it against her that she didn't come to the dinner table.

At the same time, it hurts when we do something for someone and we feel we're not appreciated. Remember, it isn't that Mom isn't grateful for what you've done, she simply doesn't remember it.

•If you live a distance from your father and he's complaining about the treatment he's receiving from family members or professional caregivers, don't jump to any conclusions. Check it out. Maybe he needs help; maybe he just doesn't remember all the good help he's getting.

•If Mom doesn't remember the things you've been doing for her, the times you've visited recently, don't scold her about it or test her. Calmly mention the meal you shared a few days earlier or the television program you enjoyed together. There's no point in trying to get her to admit she was wrong, to admit that you're helping. Just gently move on.

•Look into using respite care for your parent. This could be overnight, several hours at home during the day, or all day at an adult day center.

•Understand that part of the loss is the inability to learn new

things. Your parent is going to become more and more dependent on you.
　•Do the best you can to provide care but accept the fact that your
parent may reach a point where you're no longer able to be the primary
caregiver. Your parent may need to move to a skilled-care facility.
　•Don't be surprised if you begin to grieve before your parent
dies. One of the great heartaches of dementia is that Mom or Dad
may slip away long before his or her body quits working.

*Holy Spirit, give me hope when I feel hopeless. Be my
light when all I see, when all I feel, is darkness.*

40. Depression and Suicide

　Depression is a form of emotional illness that's treatable. If your
parent is suffering from depression — not just experiencing a
common, much less serious case of being "down in the dumps" for a
while — he or she can't will it away. Your parent can't simply
decided "I'm not going to be depressed anymore."
　And you can't just make it go away for your mother or father.
　In this chapter we're talking about your parent having
depression, but the same applies to you. As a caregiver, you're also
susceptible to becoming depressed.
　Among the commonly-accepted signs of depression are:
　• A persistent sad, anxious, or empty mood;
　• Feelings of hopelessness and pessimism, a feeling that it
　　doesn't matter what you do anymore;
　• Feelings of worthlessness, helplessness, and guilt;
　• A loss of interest in pleasure, in daily activities, and in sex;
　• Disturbed sleep, including insomnia, early waking, or
　　oversleeping;
　• Disturbed eating, including a loss of appetite, weight gain, or
　　weight loss;

•Decreased energy, constant fatigue;

•Restlessness, irritability;

•Difficulty concentrating, remembering, or making decisions;

•Thoughts of death or suicide.

Some people with depression need counseling and/or medication. They need to be educated about the cycle of depression and learn how to better cope with stress.

It may be easier for you to see the signs of depression in your parent than it is for your parent to see them in himself or herself.

If Mom has a number of the signs listed above and they persist for several weeks, you would be wise to consult with a health-care professional and share your concerns.

If Dad is showing signs of depression, it's important for him to have a physical. Depression is difficult to diagnose because there are other conditions that have some of the same symptoms. For instance, Dad may be reacting to new medication or there may be a physical condition that is causing the changes in his emotions.

Your parent may need mental health counseling and it may be difficult to get him or her to agree to that. Your parent is from a generation which, in general, isn't comfortable with that kind of care.

"I'm not crazy!" may be the argument. No one is saying Mom or Dad is. Depression and insanity are *not* the same thing, even though years ago — and even today — they're often lumped together.

Mom may be prone to depression. It may be a part of her family medical history that no one realizes, or talks about. Great-grandma had a little "breakdown." An uncle had some "trouble" for a time.

Your mother may also be more susceptible to depression if she has low self-esteem. If she feels she's not in control of things. If she sets unrealistic expectations for herself.

Her depression could be triggered by the death of her spouse, the death of one of your siblings, or a diagnosis of a chronic and debilitating illness. She may feel numb after that. Start to become less active. And gradually slide into depression.

If Dad has depression, one of the most serious and telling symptoms he may exhibit is the thought of suicide. He may talk about it, but not use that word. This isn't a natural, coming-to-the-end-of-life "I'm going to die. It may be soon." This may mean "I want out. I just can't take this anymore. I'm so tired, if I could just rest."

There is an incredibly high risk of suicide among the elderly. Experts say the actual number of suicides among the senior generation is under reported.

Unfortunately, the elderly who do try to kill themselves are usually successful.

This is important: You will *not* increase the risk of Mom committing suicide if you talk to her about it. If you ask her if she's had those thoughts or feelings. If you find out if she has a plan, a method, in mind.

It's possible to get a rough assessment on how immediate and serious the problem is based on her answers. If she talks about a gun that's in the house or about stockpiling her medication, it's one thing. If she's wheelchair-bound and talks about jumping off a bridge to which she has no access, it's another.

It goes without saying, this is all very frightening to you. To read about. To think about. What can you do to help your parent or, as we said earlier, to help yourself if you have depression? These are some suggestions:

•Become educated on what depression is and on suicide prevention.

•Make sure Mom has that physical checkup. Get her into mental health care and on the necessary medication.

•Get support for yourself. It's hard to be around someone who has depression.

•Remember, at this point, Dad doesn't have control over how he feels. He feels helpless and hopeless.

•Offer Mom support. Be strong for her. Assure her that with professional help those feelings will change. Remind her you're in this with her. She doesn't have to have it all together right now. It's the two of you *together* who are facing this problem.

•Reintroduce pleasant activities into Dad's life. Things that he considered enjoyable. *(See chapter 42 on having fun.)*

•If Mom is using a phrase that has a suicidal connotation to it, ask her point blank: "Do you have a plan?" If she's serious and has a workable plan, don't leave her alone until there's intervention by mental health professionals. These people can come to her home.

If you're talking to her on the phone, make a "contract" with her. Have her agree to not do anything until you call her back in a few minutes. Then hang up and call mental health (the local crisis line or suicide prevention phone line) to have them come to her home or call the police. When you call your mother back, keep her on the phone until help arrives.

If you feel she won't agree to a contract like that, just keep talking to her.

•Even if there is no immediate danger, talk to someone at the local crisis clinic or suicide prevention phone line. Explain what you're seeing with Dad and ask if you should be concerned. A professional can make a very quick assessment and help you with whatever steps need to be taken.

•In the area of prevention, pay particular attention to letting Mom or Dad be in control as much as possible. *(See chapter 7 on independence.)* And, of course, continue to offer the compassionate care that helps your parent lead the richest and fullest life he or she possibly can.

Emotional Health

Thank you, Lord, for all those childhood activities Mom made possible for me. Now I want to encourage her to stay active and involved.

41. The Danger of Being Too Isolated

It's called "nesting" and it's not all that uncommon.

"Nesting" refers to an older person burrowing in at home. The world shrinks to that one favorite chair in front of the television. Within reach is the TV remote, piles of old newspapers and magazines, snack food, and a coffee cup (or bottle of liquor if there's a drinking problem).

Nesting is a sure sign a parent has become too isolated, but there are other symptoms an adult child should watch for before Mom or Dad reaches this point.

What does it matter if a parent just wants to be alone? We all value our privacy, we all enjoy time by ourselves, but we humans are social animals. We need to be around others. A parent who has become — or is becoming — a hermit is in danger of fostering a host of problems.

There is truth to the maxim "use it or lose it." A person who is mentally stimulated and challenged can think more clearly. A person who gets some physical exercise, who is out and about, feels better and sleeps more soundly at night. A person who is concerned about others, who feels he or she is still making a contribution, is less self-absorbed. A person who still needs basic social skills is going to continue to pay attention to appearance and manners.

Sometimes there's a very good reason that an older person may not get out as much for a time. It could be

99

Mom has been sick. Maybe Dad is recovering from surgery. We all have — and need — our down times. For an aging parent, it's not hard for that recuperative period to blend into an unhealthy isolation.

What are some signs that your parent may be spending too much time home alone? Mom used to belong to a parish guild or altar society but now only attends Sunday Mass. Dad has let the garden go to seed. Mom no longer takes the bus downtown for that once-a-month luncheon with friends. Dad only goes out to buy groceries and he doesn't even want to do that.

Why does this happen? Maybe Mom's closest friends have died and it's not easy, not the same, making new ones. Maybe Dad is concerned that mentally he's not as quick as he used to be. He forgets names. He gets confused when he's out of the house. Maybe Mom is hiding the fact she's having trouble walking. Or gets dizzy sometimes. Or has a problem controlling her bladder.

Maybe your parent is simply afraid. The news is filled with stories of violent crimes, and your mother or father may feel vulnerable.

What can you do to help?

•Ask Dad why he doesn't want to go out. Maybe there's a very simple explanation and solution.

•Find out what community programs and activities are available for Mom. Senior Information and Assistance can help. *(See chapter 47 on finding help and "Resources" in the back of the book.)*

•Visit a local senior center with your father. Better still, visit with Dad and a friend of his. Take a tour. Have lunch there. Meet some of the other participants. Check the schedule and see what interests the two of them, what would be fun for them.

•Offer to drive Mom and pick her up from an afternoon recital or a movie matinee. Offer to find out about bus schedules, cab rates, and senior van rides.

•Encourage Dad to volunteer. To get involved in a project or program that interests him and needs his talents.

Find out what's happening at your mom's parish. Help her become more active there. Often a fellow parishioner is going to the same talk, party, or meal and is happy to act as chauffeur.

•Be on hand — as co-host and caterer — so Mom or Dad can have company over for lunch or coffee and cake.

Don't expect things to turn around overnight. Becoming too isolated is a gradual process. So is correcting the problem.

Dear God, when did having fun get to be so hard! Lord, teach us to play.

42. The Need to Have Fun

When you're caught up in the worries and demands of taking care of a parent, it's easy to overlook how important it is for your mother or father to do something enjoyable, to do something fun.

No matter how old we are, our emotional good health depends a great deal on fun. And it's especially critical when illness, depression and grief chip away at our spirits. Unfortunately, sometimes when we most need those good times, they're the first things we eliminate.

Finding and suggesting something that will be enjoyable for your parent isn't always easy. It takes imagination, work . . . and diplomacy.

These are some suggestions:

•It's important to ask Dad what he would like to do for fun, but realize your question might be met with a less than enthusiastic response. When we're out of practice having fun, attempting to do so seems a foolish idea, one that's going to take too much effort.

Whatever idea you come up with, no matter how great it may be, it could take quite a bit of low-pressure salesmanship over an extended period before your father is willing to give it a shot.

•How do you come up with ideas when Mom won't cooperate? Think about what she used to like to do. Did it have to do with traveling? Collecting? Sports? Reading? Music? What was Mom's ideal vacation? What were her plans when she first retired?

Obviously the time to do some of those things has passed. Mom won't be touring Europe. She may not be up to attending plays at the local college. The challenge then is to find another way for your parent to continue to enjoy what has interested him or her.

If Mom used to love to go to museums, find out what art books and videos are available at the library. Keep an eye out for television programs that are going to feature an artist whose work she especially admires. If it's going to be broadcast at an inconvenient time, tape it.

And then go through the book or watch the tape *with* your mother. This is especially important. The point is not for you to hand her a book or flip on the VCR and then disappear. The point is for the two of you to do this together. To talk about what you see. What you like and what you don't like. To remember trips to museums. To reminisce about favorite exhibits.

For that thirty minutes or an hour, your mother once again can be an amateur art critic. She can enjoy a pastime that gave her so much pleasure when she was younger.

•The same guidelines apply in whatever area interests your parent. If Dad loved to read murder mysteries, read one out loud to him for fifteen or twenty minutes several times throughout the day.

If he was an avid sports fan, make a point of being there with him to watch some games on television. ("Go" to the Super Bowl together.) Make a friendly wager. If his diet will allow it, serve a half-time meal of hot dogs and beer.

Find something enjoyable you two can do together on a daily or weekly basis and then stick to a schedule that gives your parent something to look forward to.

This all sounds corny because it is. A lot of what ends up being fun is corny. At first glance it seems so silly, but sometimes it's just what you and your parent need to take a break from those worries and demands and simply enjoy each other's company.

Heavenly Father, Dad has earned the right to rest. Help us find the things he would enjoy doing now.

43. Leisure-time Activities

Members of today's senior generation didn't just embrace the American work ethic; they embodied it. Year after year, decade after decade, they took great pride in giving an honest day's work for an honest day's wages.

That is, until the year, until the day, when it was time to retire. And then, sometimes abruptly, that precious and rare commodity known as free time filled their lives.

Some took a while to adjust to their new state of life. Others acted like the proverbial kid set loose in the candy store.

Defining "leisure" isn't easy. One person's job is another's hobby. In general, leisure-time activities fall into several broad categories.

•"Temporary shutdown." This is the classic couch potato. Just about everyone enjoys this from time to time, although obviously it's not good when it fills up an entire schedule.

•"Time alone." This might be reading or people-watching.

•"Creative time alone." This includes activities such as knitting or carpentry projects.

•"Service." This is simply volunteer work.

While a recent retiree may find a satisfying combination of the four for a while, that initial burst of enthusiasm doesn't always last. Then, too, as the years go by, declining health may mean adjustments have to be made.

What can you do to encourage your aging parent to keep active? Here are some recommendations:

•Understand why Dad may be doing less. It could be that an illness has become the focus of his attention for a time but as he begins to feel better, or to adjust to his new circumstances, his old hobbies should start to appeal to him again.

If not, it's important to know that a lack of interest in the things that used to give him pleasure is one of the symptoms of clinical depression. *(See chapter 40 on depression.)*

•Keep in mind that sometimes Mom may hesitate to continue a favorite pastime, or to take it up again, because she knows it's not going to be the same as it was before. Maybe she played cards with a group of friends for years and now she's the only one who hasn't moved away or died. Playing with other people, new people, just isn't the same for her. After all, it wasn't the card game that mattered. It was the companionship.

And even though your mother may want to make new friends, she hesitates. Won't they just move on, won't they die too?

•Help Mom or Dad by asking "What is it you've always wanted to do?" Follow that up by seeing to it that your parent gets whatever supplies, equipment, or instructions he or she may need.

•Check out what resources are available in the community. Some community colleges offer classes for senior at little or no cost. Senior centers provide a multitude of programs including classes, activities, meals, and socials.

•Explore with your parent what type of volunteer work he or she might enjoy doing. One organization, the Retired Senior Volunteer Program (RSVP), is listed in most phone books.

•Be careful not to fall into the trap of trying to pack your parent's schedule from dawn to dusk. Remember, the point is to encourage, not to dictate or overwhelm.

Activities of Daily Living

God, help me step back and get a clear picture of what's happening with my parent. Please give me the skills to be a good observer.

44. Assessment: What Help Does Mom or Dad *Really* Need?

Take a step back. There are times when that's the first move you need to make when trying to determine how your parent is doing. Look at the situation the way a concerned but objective outsider would.

"Mom used to be so active. . . ."

"Dad's just rattling around that big, old house. . . ."

"My parents are eating less than what I feed my preschooler. . . ."

What do you need to be looking for when you're trying to determine how your parent is doing? How your parent is *really* doing?

The bottom line is this: Is your parent safe in his or her present situation and able to do the things he or she wants to do, and if not, what steps need to be taken to make that happen?

"To do the things he or she wants to do" brings up the issue of quality of life. You need to remember it's your parent — not you, not your siblings, not your parent's siblings, not a concerned neighbor — who determines what that life will be.

Wait a minute here! If Dad refuses to go to the senior center anymore and prefers to stay home and watch "As the World Turns" and "General Hospital" every day, don't you need to step in — for his own good — and. . . .

Maybe. Maybe not. That's what assessing is all

about. It's looking carefully at each piece of the jigsaw puzzle to see the complete picture, and not simply focusing on one or two pieces. The complete picture needs to include information from four basic areas:

•physical
•mental
•emotional and
•social.

What can make the task even more difficult is trying to look at each area objectively. It may be hard to put aside emotions, and there's always the temptation to gloss over some area or need because the truth can hurt so much. ("Well, yes, Mom doesn't seem to hear everything that's said but. . . .")

And you need to base your assessment on what you see your parent doing or not doing now. ("I know Dad's always been able to. . . .")

Also, you can't dismiss an apparent problem with a handy excuse. ("If he wasn't tired today, I'm sure he could. . . .")

It's best to begin any assessment with reviewing some good, basic information on the aging process to get an idea of what's normal. For example:

•Dad says he seems to be forgetting things lately. Should I worry?
•Mom says her feet have gone numb. Is that typical?
•Dad has trouble reading the newspaper. He's just sure the print has gotten smaller. What's that mean?
•Mom used to get up at the crack of dawn. Now she's sleeping in till 8:00 or so. Is that bad?

Your parent's doctor is a good resource for basic information. So is the Area Agency on Aging. It can be contacted through Senior Information and Assistance. *(See chapter 47 on finding help and "Resources" in the back of the book.)*

If your parent has been diagnosed with a particular illness or disease and you want information of a more specific nature, contact the national association that focuses on it. Often these have a toll-free number. Call information (1-800-555-1212) and ask for any listing under that particular topic. For example, "Parkinson's Disease" or "stroke."

Once you have a basic idea of what growing old really means, you can better look at the four major areas of assessment.

Physical

Your parent needs to see a doctor for a complete physical examination, and you both need to listen to what the physician recommends.

You need a good — meaning clear — diagnosis. Hearing "It might be this or it might be that or it might be something else" isn't going to help. You need to ask about the prognosis. (The diagnosis is the identifying of the disease from its signs and symptoms. The prognosis is a forecast of what's going to happen because of that particular problem. For example, how long will this symptom last? Will other complications and problems follow? How soon? Will there be a rapid deterioration in health or a gradual one?)

Your parent's hearing and vision also need to be tested.

And take a look at your parent's daily routine. How is Mom sleeping? Has she lost weight recently? Is she smoking? Has she been drinking more? Should she be drinking at all with the current medication she's taking?

What medications is Dad on now? If he has more than one doctor prescribing more than one medication, does each doctor know what the other has given him?

What about mobility? Can Mom get up from a chair and walk around? Does she need some adaptive equipment, a walker or cane?

Is there a problem with incontinence, the loss of bowel control, or more commonly, bladder control? This is difficult to talk about. Although there are more television ads praising the benefits of adult protective wear, the subject is still taboo in many households. Yes, it can be extremely embarrassing to have to ask or answer questions about incontinence but it needs to be done. And done respectfully.

Finally, listen when your parent tells you his or her symptoms. It may be that day after day, week after week, it's the same litany of minor aches and pains or of problems already being addressed, but there could be something new in there. Something that needs immediate attention.

Mental

How is your parent's memory, both long- and short-term? Does

Dad seem confused? Can he remember Christmas 1955 but forget to eat? Can he still handle his own finances? Can he make and stick to a decision or does he seem able to say yes and no in the same sentence and mean both?

Is Mom showing poor judgment? Did she leave the front door wide open all night — in a very unsafe neighborhood — because it was hot out?

Does she know what day it is? What time of day?

Can she follow a conversation? Does she seem to have trouble with her receptive language ability? (Her ability to understand the words you use and follow the general train of thought in everyday conversations.) Is there a problem with her expressive language? (Does she use the wrong word or seem unable to come up with a word for which she's searching?)

Is she aware of her mistakes, and do they make her feel frightened and angry? Or is she oblivious to them?

Is there evidence of dementia — cognitive loss — a deterioration in mental ability? Do you need to arrange for a professional assessment?

Emotional

Again, what do you see? Is Mom depressed quite a bit of the time? Does she not want to get up in the morning? Does she complain of having no energy? Does she burst into tears?

Is she using suicidal phrases? Does she say things like "Life's not worth living anymore." "I don't want to be here." "What's the point?" "It's going to be over soon." "It would be better if I just died."

Is she grieving? Has she recently suffered a major loss? (The death of a spouse, failing health, an amputation and so on.) Does she seem angry all the time? Frustrated? Resistant to any help?

Is she frightened most of the time? Is she generally anxious or agitated? Is she afraid to stay alone at night or does she panic when you say you have to leave?

Has her mood been taking wide swings, from extremely angry to completely passive?

Social

Does it seem that Dad is becoming more and more isolated from the rest of the world? Does he get out and see other people as much as he wants to? Have telephone calls and letter writing replaced visits, and is he content with that?

How does he spend his leisure time? Does he just sit in front of the television for most of the day? Does he have any hobbies? Does he have a pet?

Is he just not interested in anything anymore or has he adjusted his interests to match his abilities? (For example, he used to love gardening but now he reads gardening magazines and watches gardening shows on TV.)

If both your parents are still living, is there more stress, more friction, between Mom and Dad?

Does Dad know what he needs and if so, can he get it for himself? If he wants to go someplace, can he figure out how to get there — by walking or driving, by taking a bus or taxi, or by arranging for someone to drive him?

Is he still involved at his church? If he can't make it to Sunday Mass, can he arrange for someone from his parish to stop by the house with Communion?

An evaluator's checklist

There may be a major concern in one of the four areas that obviously needs to be addressed first. It could be that nothing stands out, but there are a lot of little problems which, added together, may mean a parent *isn't* safe and he or she needs some kind of help immediately.

A social worker evaluating a senior's living situation considers the individual's "activities of daily living." Without help, can she:

- eat,
- walk,
- use the toilet,
- take a bath, and
- get dressed?

And the evaluator looks at "instrumental activities of daily living." Can he:

- handle the finances,
- go shopping,
- drive the car or take the bus,

•do the housework and laundry,
•prepare meals, and
•take the right amount of the right
    medication at the right time?

Once needs are determined — and sometimes it's best to do this with that outside, more objective help — then you can investigate how those needs can begin to be met by family, friends, neighbors, people from the parish, and professionals.

Keep in mind that *those needs may fluctuate.* Mom may have to have someone in to help with the cooking and cleaning for a while after her surgery but later she can resume those duties. Dad might have had no trouble paying the bills six months ago, but recently there have been a lot of extra charges for late payments.

Assessing a parent's need isn't a one-time task. It's a job that needs to be repeated periodically to make sure you're seeing all the little pieces in order to get a clear view of the big picture: your parent's health, safety, and quality of life.

Guardian angels, watch over Mom when I can't. Protect her from harm.

45. Personal Safety

It isn't just the elderly who need to be concerned about the current increase in crime but, unfortunately, frequently they're its victims.

A robber or burglar is looking for the easiest target that will yield the best results. Often it's an aging parent who fits that category. It's Mom or Dad who becomes the prey.

What can you do to help keep your parent safe? Here are some suggestions:

•Law enforcement officers say one of the best things an older person, or anyone of any age, can do to protect himself or herself is pay attention when out in public. To walk purposefully. To look like a strong and uninviting target.

•But they say, that doesn't mean playing the hero. If someone demands or grabs for a purse or wallet, let it go. Its contents aren't worth being injured. And for an aging parent, a punch or push could easily lead to broken bones or worse.

•They also warn, in a reversal of what was recommended in years past, a woman should *not* have her purse strap draped around her neck. That doesn't stop today's thief. It only increases the likelihood the victim will be hurt as well as robbed.

•Also, Mom shouldn't be out in public wearing a lot of expensive jewelry. That's inviting trouble.

•If your parent is still receiving pension or Social Security checks through the mail, arrange for direct deposit at the bank.

•Go shopping with your parent and see how he or she does. Does Mom leave her purse unattended in the shopping cart? Does Dad flash the cash in his wallet when he's at the checkout stand? We all need reminders when it comes to personal safety. We all slip into what can be dangerous habits. Tell your parent what you see. What a would-be robber will see.

•If Dad still drives, make sure his car is well maintained. This decreases the odds it will break down at a time or place that isn't safe. Also, be sure he keeps all the doors locked.

•Find out if there's a security escort to the parking lot at the hospital or doctor's clinic, at the mall and so on.

•Remind Mom crime happens day and night now. She needs to be alert whenever she goes out.

•Walk around your father's house to make sure the doors and windows can be and are securely locked. Cut back shrubs that could shield someone attempting to break in. Make sure the porch light works and that there's a peephole in the door at the right height so it will be used. Have your dad keep the screen or storm door locked, too. Remind him *never* to open the door to a stranger.

•Help your parent understand that the old neighborhood may have changed since the family first moved there. It may no longer be safe to walk to the grocery store or church. Offer to give or arrange a ride.

•Remind Mom not to give out any personal information over the phone unless she knows the caller. The elderly are favorite targets for phone fraud. Your state attorney general's office can offer tips on how to help your parent avoid getting stung.

•Have Dad be part of the Block Watch program and report any suspicious activity in the neighborhood. Find out what tips the program offers for making your parent's community and home safer. You could also ask a trusted neighbor to keep an eye on Dad's house (and keep a respectful eye on him, too).

•Don't let fear keep Mom or Dad — or you — from enjoying life. The solution isn't to become a hermit. The answer is to use caution and common sense.

Holy Spirit, be my guide when I have to make decisions and I'm not sure what's best for Mom.

46. Choosing the Best Solution

It's not unusual for an adult child taking care of an aging parent to discover an unexpected problem has a number of possible solutions.

After looking carefully at your parent's needs and the various ways to meet those needs, it may become clear that there is no single right or wrong choice. There may be many choices, each with merit.

So which is best for Mom or Dad? How can you be sure you and your parent are making the right decision?

The following are basic principles commonly used in the field of social work when assisting an elderly person. It can help a family to consider each when trying to reach a decision.

•You're dealing with a whole person, not simply one or two particular problems. It doesn't mean Mom is doing well just because she has a safe place to live and is eating all right.

For example, what about her health in general? Is she receiving proper care?

What about her need to get out and socialize? Does she have the opportunity to be a part of the community?

What about her spiritual needs? Can she get to Mass? Does she still feel as if she's part of the parish?

•An elderly person still has the right to be treated with dignity and respect. A solution should not humiliate or embarrass Mom or Dad. Your parent's privacy should continue to be respected.

•Your parent is an individual. Avoid cookie-cutter approaches. Just because one particular choice worked best for your neighbor's aging parent doesn't automatically mean the same will be best for yours. Just because one solution was the best fit for Dad five years ago doesn't automatically make it right for Mom today.

It's so easy for a family to fall into the trap of thinking, "This is how we did it with Grandma, so this must be how we need to do with Mom." Not necessarily. Yes, it *may* be the best way, but then again, it may not.

To use another comparison, the best-fitting solutions, like the best-fitting suits, are tailor-made, not bought off the rack or hand-me-downs.

•It's important your father is involved in the decision making and that means keeping him informed when information is being gathered. He should participate in the entire process.

It also means there are no secrets. It is not uncommon for a family to want to hide or disguise the cost of a particular service (home care, for example) because Dad won't like it. Invariably, keeping secrets, withholding information, or telling little white lies backfires. *(See chapter 67 on keeping secrets.)*

•Closely related to that participation, is self-determination. This means that, even if you *strongly* disagree with Mom, she maintains the right to make her own decisions.

There are exceptions when intervention is necessary, such as severe dementia or attempted suicide, but remember the exceptions are rare, not the norm. Just because you don't like your Mom's choice doesn't mean she no longer has the right to make that choice.

Perhaps no solution will perfectly match all five principles, but often the best choice for your parent is the one that comes closest.

Show me where to turn, Lord. Lead me to the people, the agencies, and the programs that will be best for my parent.

47. Finding Help for Your Parent

You've reached the point where you know your parent needs more help than you alone can provide, and you want to assist Mom or Dad in getting that help. Now what do you do?

Typically, this will be easier if both you and your parent live in the same area. Calls are local and you can have personal contact with the people who will be working with him or her.

On the other hand, living nearby often means making more of a time commitment to get things started and to monitor them once they're going. There can be a greater danger of your becoming overly involved and burning out.

If you live near your parent, a good first step is to call Senior Information and Assistance, which is listed in the phone book. The person there can tell you what private and public social service programs are in the area.

These would include, for example, home health care (visiting nurse, bath aid); home care (housekeeping, laundry, grocery shopping); transportation; and nutrition service programs, such as Meals on Wheels.

But what if you and your parent live in different parts of the country?

By law, according to the Older Americans Act, every state must be able to provide information about services for the elderly living there.

A service called the Eldercare Locator (1-800-677-1116) can give you, without charge, the Senior Information and Assistance number for anywhere in the United States. All they need is your parent's ZIP code.

Senior Information and Assistance can send you a list of private and public social service programs for the region in which your parent lives. *(See "Resources" in the back of the book.)* Also, it can provide information on local case managers.

The use of a case manager is something to consider whether you live near your parent or not. *(See chapter 49 on hiring a case manager.)* This is a social worker who can help you investigate what options are available for your parent and can help Mom or Dad sign up to receive services.

Whether you use a case manager or not, it's important to keep an eye out for what else is being offered. As you begin to find out what help is available for your parent's particular needs and wants, you may realize there are other areas in your parent's everyday life where he or she needs assistance. Perhaps six months or a year from now your parent will have an additional need and you'll have a better idea of how it can be met.

Financial help is another point to keep in mind. With some programs, an elderly person does not have to fall into a low-income bracket to receive low- or no-cost services. Don't shy away from a program because, at first glance, it seems too expensive. It may in fact use a sliding-fee scale.

All of the above may be considered the formal support network for your parent, but don't forget the informal network. This includes other family members as well as your parent's friends, neighbors, and fellow parishioners.

Often those most pleased to help (to be asked to help) are the ones who have an elderly family member in another part of the country who is benefiting from his or her own informal network. They know how much that help has meant not only to their relative, but to them.

*Lord, some challenges are harder than others.
This one isn't easy.*

48. When Your Parent Needs Help Bathing

To put it bluntly, your parent may not be bathing as often as he or she should and may have strong body odor.

As Mom ages and becomes more frail, it may be more difficult for her to step in and out of a bathtub, to maintain her balance, to towel off. Her fear of falling increases, and rightly so.

However, forcing the issue by marching her into the bathroom and pushing her through the process isn't just disrespectful, it's also dangerous. It may increase the likelihood of her slipping and falling.

What can you do?

•Understand that modesty, embarrassment, and independence each play a role in why Dad may not want or ask for help bathing. Lifelong modesty says that's something that's done alone. Coupled with that may be some embarrassment about how his body has aged and how it looks now. And tied to both is the sad truth that the inability to take a bath or a shower without help is another milestone on the road toward dependence on others, a milestone anyone would want to postpone.

Even if your father has accepted help in other areas, realize that having someone come in and vacuum the living room carpet once a week is not the same as having someone come in to give him a bath.

•Keep in mind Mom may not realize she has body odor. Telling her isn't easy; not telling her isn't right.

•Remember that you can take small steps toward the goal of having someone help your parent. Maybe Dad would agree to at least have another person in the house when it's bath time. Next may be having that person help him get in and out the tub. Help him by handing him a towel. Help him with drying off or getting dressed. Maybe the final step will be helping him with the actual washing.

Sometimes it's easier to have a stranger assist your parent — someone coming in just to help — rather than relying on a family member. *(See "Resources" in the back of the book.)*

Often a good time to introduce the idea is after a parent has returned from a stay in the hospital, where, as we all know, privacy is sometimes at a minimum.

Here are a few other points to consider:

•Daily bathing is a recent phenomenon. Many people grew up with the idea of a weekly bath.

•An elderly person has sensitive skin that needs a good rinsing but not necessarily a lot of soap and certainly not heavy scrubbing.

•A bathtub's safety features should include a bath bench or bath chair (available from medical-supply stores); a hand-held shower head; a grab bar bolted into the studs of the wall (not just a towel rack); and a good bath mat.

•And a last but very important point: **Make sure the hot water heater in your parent's home is set below 120 degrees.** Sensitive skin can be burned in only a few short seconds.

Lord, thank you for the people who work so hard taking care of others. Help me find the right one for my parent.

49. Hiring a Case Manager

(This chapter looks at how a case manager can help if you're a long-distance caregiver; however, even if you and your parent live near one another, the service may be worth considering. You and your parent may be in the same area, but the demands of your job or children may make it impossible for you to help out as much as you would like to right now. Or maybe you can't be a "front-line" caregiver because, in the past, your parent was abusive. Perhaps you simply don't know where to start to look for the help your parent needs. Hiring a case manager may be the solution.)

"What am I going to find this time?" That's a question that can hound an adult child traveling a distance to visit an aging parent. An adult child who's able to make it back home only every year or two. *(See chapters 71 and 72 on long-distance caregiving.)*

How is Mom really doing? How much ground has Dad lost in the last twelve months?

Walking in the front door can tell you more than almost any phone call, any letter. Spending a day with your parent can make his or her condition clear.

That's when the emotions kick in. The fear, panic almost. The urge to fix everything immediately. The overwhelming guilt.

Why did I wait so long between visits? Why didn't I pick up on these problems when we talked on the phone or wrote? Why do I live so far away? Why didn't I stay closer to home, where I belong, where I could *do* something?

Then, too, for the long-distance son or daughter, there's the summons. Mom has had a stroke. Dad has had a heart attack. Come home *now*. Come home and handle all these details. All these problems.

What do you do? After all, in a week or two — at the most — you need to be back at work. Back taking care of your own family. Back at your own home that's hundreds or thousands of miles away.

A solid first step is to have an honest assessment of your parent's present condition. *(See chapter 44 on assessment.)* There are professionals who can do this with you.

Consider your parent's physical well-being. How is her health in general? Is she eating right? Is she being treated by a doctor? Is she taking her medication properly? Drinking too much?

How is your parent's mental health? Is he confused sometimes? Does he have some memory loss?

Consider his or her emotional well being. Is she depressed? Suicidal?

What about safety issues? Is his house or apartment safe from intruders? From fire? From falls? What about the neighborhood?

What about your parent's daily-living routine? Should she quit driving? Can she get around on the bus? Is her home clean? Can she do her own laundry, shopping, bathing, and cooking?

If you have concerns, consider hiring a case manager

(sometimes called care manager) who can watch over your parent after you're back home.

Typically a case manager is a social worker or registered nurse. You can find out about local services through Senior Information and Assistance. *(See chapter 47 on finding help and "Resources" in the back of the book.)*

Case managers' fees vary from no cost to as much as $100 an hour. It pays to shop around. The most expensive is not necessarily the one that will best fit your needs. And a "bargain" may not be one at all.

Find out what several case managers offer and check out their credentials and references. Do they have a social work or medical focus? Will they be in contact with you on a regular basis or are you supposed to check in with them to find out what's happening?

As much a possible, bring your parent in on the process. Let Mom or Dad meet this person. If there's a strong personality clash, it's probably not going to work with that individual.

Keep in mind a case manager will not clean your parent's house, won't drive Dad to the doctor or give Mom a bath, but will set up services to see to it these things get done.

If your parent's condition worsens, services can be added. (Even to the point of placement in a nursing home.) If it improves, they can be modified or dropped.

A good case manager can be your eyes and ears. He or she can make sure your mother or father is receiving the care that's needed and put your own mind more at ease, too.

Jesus, help me be gentle but firm.

50. When Mom or Dad Doesn't Want Help

There may be times when Mom simply says "no." When Dad wants *nothing* to do with what you're proposing. You may have come up with what you think is a great solution to whatever problem or need your parent is facing, but your mother or father doesn't see it that way.

Not by a long shot.

And so Dad digs in his heels or Mom gets that look in her eyes, and you know it's going to take a lot of work on your part to get your parent to budge on this one.

What can you do to avoid that kind of confrontation?

•It helps to talk about concerns — early and often — out in the open. It's much easier to hold "what if" discussions before a crisis arises. "What if you needed some help around the house. . .?" "What if you couldn't safely drive anymore. . .?" What could your parent do, what could you do, what could someone else do to help out? What are other people both of you know doing or not doing in these situations?

•If there's already a need, don't present "the solution" — meaning your choice. Try to give Mom or Dad a number of possibilities. Let your parent decide. If your parent isn't mentally competent, get professional help to assist you in planning and making necessary decisions.

•If there's any resistance, go with the minimum service first. Maybe Mom doesn't want someone in her home four hours every day but she'll agree to a person coming in for two hours a week to help with the cleaning or laundry. Then as she and the worker get to know one another, the idea of increasing those hours and the workload may not be nearly as threatening.

•Remember, your goal is not to take over your parent's life but to assist him or her in getting what's needed. This can be done without trampling on Mom's or Dad's right to choose. This can be done while continuing to show great love — and respect — for your parent.

Technical Matters

Heavenly Father, help me be a wise steward with Dad's money. He worked so hard all his life. Thank you for the example he set.

51. Financial Issues

Taking over your parent's finances might be as difficult for Mom or Dad as giving up the car keys. Often it's seen as an assault on his or her independence. It's easy to understand why it may be met with resistance.

Still, it may be that Mom or Dad needs your help even if, at times, it isn't wanted. Or much appreciated.

Your parent is probably anxious about finances. *(See chapter 4 on two common life experiences.)* Mom is afraid that eventually all her money is going to be used up and she'll find herself destitute. She's saving that money for her "old age."

She has a point. It's important you do some research to find out not only how much is coming in, but how much is likely to be going out. Income can be from a variety of sources: Social Security, pension, insurance, savings, investments, and so on. Estimated expenses need to be realistic, to reflect inflation and the added costs that are likely to crop up as your parent grows older.

Discussing finances is never easy. It's not unusual for siblings to have different opinions on how best to proceed. To have different, strongly-held opinions. It's important to avoid turning the task into a turf war and, instead, to concentrate on doing what's best for your parent.

These are some suggestions:

•Know where your parent's financial records are kept. This is especially important if there is any dementia.

A demented person sometimes puts items in very inappropriate places. A will might be in the back of the freezer. A bank book in an old box of cat food.

•If you're handling Mom's finances, keep extremely good records. Write everything down. Sometimes a parent with dementia will accuse an adult child of "stealing" money.

•Consider having an accountant handle this chore right from the beginning. An accountant can be the one to review your parent's assets and make suggestions for getting the best return on investments.

•You need a good money-management plan for your parent's resources. The American Association of Retired Persons (AARP) has information on that. *(See "Resources" in the back of the book.)*

•Remember your parent may be eligible for a number of federal or state services even if he or she is not low-income. An example would be respite care.

•Make sure your parent has a will, that you know who the executor is, and that you know where the will is located.

Lord, help me get through the maze of legal terms and choices and find what's best for Dad.

52. Legal Terms and Senior Health Care

This subject — end-of-life decisions — may be very difficult to discuss with your parent because it's so packed with emotions. At the same time, talking about this can make things much easier for both your parent and you during the final days of your parent's life when these decisions are needed.

When talking with Mom, stress the fact that you want to respect and fulfill her wishes so you need to know what her decisions are.

You may find Dad doesn't want to discuss these things with

you. In that case, encourage him to talk about them with someone else that he trusts, someone who can be his representative.

Remember, too, that your assistance can make these decisions and preparations easier for your parent. Your mother or father needs not only basic legal and medical information, but your respectful care and support.

The following isn't legal advice. These are simply legal terms that are used regarding a patient's rights and health care.

The Patient Self-determination Act: This is a federal law that guarantees you, the patient, have the right to confidentiality and the right to make your own health-care decisions. Any health-care provider (doctor, hospital, nursing home, home-care service, and so on) that receives Medicare or Medicaid funds is supposed to give this information to its patients.

Informed consent (or informed refusal): No one can force you to undergo a certain medical treatment without your approval, and before you decide, a health-care provider must give you information regarding the diagnosis, the nature and purpose of the treatment, any risks or consequences of the treatment, the probability that the treatment will be successful, any feasible alternative treatments, and the prognosis if you choose not to receive the treatment.

Living will: (Also known as an advance directive or *directive to physician*): This health-care directive is a document stating your wishes regarding life-sustaining treatment at the final stages of your life. It takes effect in the event that you are no longer able to make medical decisions. It needs to be dated and signed in the presence of two witnesses. A witness cannot be the health-care provider or someone who will benefit in some way from your death.

You can amend the information in your living will at any time and the directives it contains can be very specific.

You need to talk to your doctor and tell him or her what you want and don't want, and ask how that will be handled. Your doctor must tell you what he or she will do. If you are asking for something that your doctor refuses to do, your physician must refer you to another doctor who agrees to carry out your wishes.

No one can force you to sign a living will.

Regulations regarding advanced directives vary from state to state. If you spend part of the year in one state and part in another, set up the directives in both.

Mentally incapacitated: This can be a temporary or permanent condition leaving you unable to make a choice or make your choice known. A judge or court — not a doctor or family member — is needed to declare you mentally incapacitated, in which case a legal guardian can be assigned. This could be a family member, friend, or court-appointed advocate.

If you are declared mentally incapacitated, there is a priority system regarding who can make decisions for you. In descending order, they are: legal guardian, people with your durable power of attorney, spouse, adult children, parent, and siblings.

Durable power of attorney: This is a document that gives someone else, chosen by you, the power to make decisions for you even if you become mentally incapacitated. Most durable powers of attorney for health care take effect only if you lose the ability to make your own decisions because of illness or injury, but this depends on how the document is written.

For more information on legal terms call Senior Information and Assistance. (*See chapter 47 on finding help and "Resources" in the back of the book.*)

Spirituality

Father, Son, and Spirit, help me remember to pray.

53. Turning to Prayer

It seems strange to say it's possible for something good to come out of something as terrible as an aging parent's ever-worsening condition. But it's true. It can.

Caught up in everyday living, it's easy to forget — and to ignore — what's important. What really matters. Taking care of an aging parent changes that. Being a caregiver brings you face to face with mortality.

It's not surprising then that an aging parent and an adult child can be drawn toward prayer. If this hasn't been a central part of your parent's life or your life for a time (if ever), praying may feel awkward. Just the thought of praying may make you feel uncomfortable. How do you start? What do you say? Are you being hypocritical?

Even if you're accustomed to praying, this may be different. Maybe prayer has always been something very personal and private for you and for your parent, but now you two would like to pray together.

Where to begin?

Prayer has been defined as lifting the mind and the heart to God. That's easier to do when your mind is filled with concern for a loved one. When your heart is breaking as you watch him or her slip away.

Praying isn't complicated. There are no formulas that have to be followed. "Thee" and "thou" aren't necessary. Praying is telling God, "This is what's on my mind. This is why my heart is aching."

It's turning to the one who created your parent, to the one who *loves your parent even more than you do* — and that doesn't seem possible! — and asking for help, for comfort, for strength.

Your prayers may change as your parent's condition goes through stages. The focus of your prayers may shift. That's all right. For a time it may be "heal Mom." And that might happen. At another time it may become, "Yes, I know she's going to die, but just not now. Please. Later." And you may reach a point in your prayers when you ask God, "Let her go peacefully. When it's her time, let her go and welcome her into heaven."

But there may also be periods when what is happening is so overwhelming — so frightening, so awful — that your own words just won't come. Many adult children in that situation have discovered silently repeating the prayers they learned as children — the Our Father, the Hail Mary — can bring comfort. Some who haven't said the Rosary for years are surprised to find that this may be especially helpful. *(See "Prayers and How to Say the Rosary" in the back of the book.)*

If your parent wants to pray out loud with you, saying an Our Father or Hail Mary — or a Rosary if your mother or father has the strength — can be a good place to begin. Also, keep in mind prayers on audio tape are available at Catholic book stores. It's easier than worrying about coming up with the "right" words or avoiding the "wrong" ones.

Your parent may surprise you with the number of prayers and hymns he or she remembers. It's not uncommon that someone with a significant short-term memory loss can easily, and happily, recall what he or she memorized as a child.

It also helps to keep in mind a personal shared prayer doesn't have to be long or complicated. "Heavenly Father, bless Dad and me. Thank you for letting us be a part of each other's lives. Give us strength for whatever lies ahead."

Even if your family has never been the touching-hugging type, holding hands with your parent as you pray may feel right, may be very comforting, for both of you.

Then, too, there may be times when it helps to turn to silent prayer. For you, or for your parent, to pray privately. Again, it may be holding Mom's hand or sitting beside Dad's bed as he sleeps and, in silence, telling God what you're thinking and what you're feeling. Asking for, listening for, God's voiceless words of comfort and encouragement.

Although Catholics traditionally haven't been strong on privately reading the Bible, this is another kind of spoken prayer you both might find helpful. Don't worry about which edition you use. Try something from one of the gospels: Matthew, Mark, Luke, or John. They're filled with Jesus' words of love.

And it may be your parent has a particular rosary, medal, crucifix, or prayer book he or she wants to have nearby and go with him or her to the hospital or nursing home.

But what if you don't feel like praying and your parent asks you to? Do it, if only as a favor to Mom or Dad. It probably means a lot to your parent. And, later, after your mother or father is gone, having prayed together may mean a lot to you.

Are you being hypocritical if you turn to prayer now? No. Just the opposite. You're being true to how you feel. People change. What you're going through is changing you in many ways. It shouldn't be surprising that the change includes spiritually.

Good Shepherd, thank you for never giving up on any of your sheep.

54. Returning to the Church

People leave the Catholic Church for a variety of reasons. Some storm out. Others drift away.

Returning to the Church may be something you or your parent wants to look into now but neither of you is sure how to go about it.

A first step would be talking to a local priest. How do you find him? Check the phone directory and call the parish in your area or your parent's area.

In most parishes, the days of visiting a priest by simply knocking on the rectory door have passed. The current shortage of priests means parishes that used to have two, three, or even more priests assigned to them may now have only one. Or may not even have a priest in residence.

Don't be surprised if you get an answering service if you're calling at some time other than business hours (yes, business hours). Most likely you will be asked to leave your name and number and a brief message. Even during the day, you may need to leave a message with the parish office secretary.

This may feel very awkward, especially if you're not really sure why you're calling in the first place. If you're not really sure this is something you want to pursue.

It's enough to simply say, "My name is. . . . I'm interested (or my parent is interested) in finding out about returning to the Church." Or "I have (my parent has) some questions and would like to talk to a priest." You might also add what time of day it's easiest to reach you.

What can you expect when the priest returns your call? Someone who wants to help you. Someone who would like to warmly welcome you back.

What *won't* you get? Accusations designed to make you feel guilty. A scolding. A cold shoulder. A sales pitch for a monetary contribution to the parish. A demand that you — on the spot — make a firm commitment to return to the Church.

If Mom is homebound or in a hospital or nursing home, the priest will visit her there. He'll answer her questions and, if it's been a while since she's been an active Catholic, he may briefly explain what changes have taken place in the Church and why they've happened.

If there's a concern about a second marriage without having had the first one annulled, he'll begin to help facilitate that, too.

Maybe Dad just wants to talk. That's fine. If he wants to go to confession, he'll be given the opportunity to do that. And to receive Communion. If he's in immediate danger of death, the priest — with your parent's permission — will administer the sacrament of the anointing of the sick. *(See chapters 55-57 on reconciliation, Holy Communion, and anointing of the sick.)*

It's understandable if your parent is (or you are) nervous about this. But there's no need to be afraid. It may help to remember the priest is there to help you and your parent. Certainly one of the great joys of his vocation, his ministry, is this very thing: Welcoming back someone who has been away for a time. It's helping that person better prepare for an eternal homecoming.

Dear Jesus, thank you for giving us this way of finding peace.

55. The Sacrament of Reconciliation
(Penance, Confession)

It's not unusual that the anointing of the sick is administered in conjunction with the sacrament of reconciliation (penance or confession) and reception of the Eucharist (Holy Communion).

Sometimes people hesitate to go to confession because it has been a long time since they've been. Because they feel they've committed unforgivable sins or are afraid they can't remember everything they need to confess. Because they don't want to tell their sins "outside the box" where the priest can see them. Because, with all the changes in the Church in the last thirty years, they aren't sure how they're supposed to go to confession now. Because they can't remember the Act of Contrition.

Your parent may not even bring up the subject of going to confession but may appreciate it if you do. It's good to remind Mom or Dad:

•If it's been a long time since your parent last celebrated this sacrament, then it's a great time to do it again. The priest isn't going to scold him or her.

•No sin is unforgivable. Nothing Dad says is going to shock the priest.

•Mom doesn't need to remember a complete list of all the wrong she has done or worry about forgetting something. For example: "There were times I was angry when I shouldn't have been" rather than "On this day, I got mad at this person. On that day, I got mad at that person" and so on.

•The priest, in Jesus' name, offers forgiveness and peace. Offers God's grace. It can be wonderful to receive that face-to-face.

•Dad doesn't have to worry about how to go to confession. Again, the priest will be happy to gently lead him through it.

•An act of contrition can be as simple as "I'm sorry." Your mother doesn't need to recite the exact prayer, word for word, she learned as a child.

In recent years this sacrament hasn't been used much and that's too bad. Even if your parent doesn't want to celebrate reconciliation, consider going yourself.

The list of things you can say to your parent about this sacrament applies to you as well.

This source of grace — of spiritual strength and blessing — can make a tremendous difference in your life, especially at this time in your role as a caregiver.

My Lord and my God, thank you for being here with me.

56. Eucharist
(Holy Communion)

If you call the local parish and ask that your parent receive Communion at home (or in the hospital or nursing home), it's likely that a lay Eucharistic minister will be the one who visits.

You will also be welcome to go to Communion at that time. The rules for fasting (no food or drink, except water, for one hour) don't apply for your parent.

As with the anointing of the sick, don't worry about setting up for a sick call. The volunteer from the parish will bring whatever he or she needs or ask in advance if you can supply something (a candle, for example).

Typically, the prayers the Eucharistic minister says will seem like an abridged version of the Mass. If you're at home, there is a penitential rite, a scriptural reading, prayers of the faithful, the Our Father, and then reception of Communion. That's followed by a closing prayer.

If in a hospital or nursing home, there's only a greeting, the Our Father, Communion, and a closing prayer.

You or your parent may choose a particular scriptural reading if you wish — Mom or Dad's favorite, for instance, or one you or your parent find especially comforting.

Let the Eucharistic minister know if your parent has trouble swallowing. He or she can break off a tiny piece of a host and give it to your mom or dad. And if your parent needs a drink of water to help with swallowing, that's all right, too. In the hospital, always check with a nurse first to make sure it's all right for your parent to have water.

Obviously, turn off any radio or television during the Communion service. And, if possible, put the telephone answering machine on or leave the handset off the cradle. Even the longer version of the service takes only five minutes or so.

With most parishes it's possible to arrange for a Eucharistic minister to visit your parent on a regular basis. Don't worry about straightening up the house for this visitor or offering coffee or a snack. The Eucharistic minister knows this isn't a social call.

And don't be concerned if the volunteer shows up at the same time a visiting nurse or other health-care provider has to be there. The parish volunteer knows these scheduling conflicts can come up unexpectedly and will simply wait until it's his or her turn.

God the Creator, bless Dad's head and hands. Bring comfort to this man who taught me so much, this man who held me close.

57. Anointing of the Sick
("Extreme Unction," "Last Rites")

In years gone by, one of the final things a family would do for a dying loved one was notify the local priest. He would hurry to the house or hospital and administer the "last rites."

In general, the sacrament, then known as extreme unction (final anointing), was reserved for someone on his or her deathbed. Since the Second Vatican Council (1962-1965), that's no longer the case.

Now known as the anointing of the sick or sacrament of the sick, it's commonly administered to anyone who has reached "the age of reason" (around seven) who is seriously ill. And it's also available for anyone who is elderly. In either case, *the recipient does not have to be near death.*

It's important to explain this to your mother or father. "Calling the priest" does *not* mean he or she is dying. It does *not* mean your dad is in worse shape than he realizes or that you're keeping some information about your mom's medical condition from her.

It's also important to know the anointing of the sick isn't a "magical" sacrament designed to cure illness. Yes, sometimes a person does get well. But the purpose of the sacrament is to give the person grace and to forgive his or her sins.

In administering the sacrament, the priest will anoint your parent's forehead and hands with blessed oil (usually olive oil) and say some prayers. You, and others, are welcome to be present.

A person can receive this sacrament more than once. If you aren't sure if it would be appropriate for your parent to be anointed, ask your local priest.

Years ago there were special crucifixes that held candles and holy water that were to be used for "sick calls." Don't worry about this. The priest will bring everything he needs.

Saints in heaven, pray for us.

58. Eternal Life: The Communion of Saints

The Catholic Church's teaching on the communion of saints can be very consoling as your parent nears death. It can be very comforting after he or she has died.

It says you can pray for, and pray to, your departed parent. You can ask for your mother's or father's help. Your parent can pray for and help you.

It says love is more powerful than the grave. It says the relationship you share doesn't have to end. Your love goes beyond death.

The communion of saints isn't referring to only those holy men and women who have been canonized, who have been declared "saints." Rather, it's the faithful who are still on earth, the souls who have gone to heaven (and the angels there), and the departed who are in purgatory.

Purgatory may seem like an old-fashioned or outdated concept. In a nutshell, it's the "purifying" of those saved souls who haven't yet entered heaven. Those who aren't yet ready, aren't yet worthy, to enter. What's it like? It's been called harsh and sweet. Harsh because becoming a more loving soul, realizing and admitting past sins, is never easy. And sweet because a soul in purgatory knows it's going to heaven.

The traditional terms for the three different groups are the Church militant (the faithful on earth), the Church suffering (the souls in purgatory) and the Church triumphant (the souls in heaven).

What does this mean for you and your parent?

It means that as Dad says good-bye to you and his family on earth, loved ones in heaven are preparing to greet him, and, with the angels, to welcome him. To bring him home.

It means that, trusting in God's mercy, Mom — following her death — may spend time further getting ready to enter her heavenly reward. And as she does, you can continue to pray for her. You can continue to help her.

It means that in heaven, from heaven, your parent still loves you. Your parent can ask God to bless you, to watch over you, to give you strength and comfort. Your parent can ask God to help you find your way. Your parent can ask God to lead you toward that incredible day when, once again, you and your parent will be together. Together forever.

The Caregiver's Life

*Sometimes my life feels like a tug-of-war, Lord.
And I'm the rope.*

59. The Sandwich Generation

The "sandwich generation" is a good description.
There's pressure from both sides and sometimes it gets
messy in the middle. That's what it can feel like if you're
taking care of not only your children but your aging parent
as well.

Add in a spouse and a job and it's no wonder it often
seems a twenty-four-hour day and seven-day week just
aren't enough for all you have to do.

Then, too, from the time all of us were little we were
taught there is a right way and a wrong way to accomplish
a task. To meet — and overcome — a challenge. Maybe
your parent took care of Grandma or Grandpa. Your
spouse took care of your mother- or father-in-law. Your
friends or co-workers seem to be able to handle their
situations. But you. . . .

When you realize, when it becomes so painfully
obvious, you can't do all the things you're supposed to do
— all the things other people have done or are doing —
you feel so inadequate. So guilty.

You think you're letting everyone down. If you just
worked a little harder. Slept a little less. Sacrificed a little
more. Then somehow. . . .

If you find yourself in that situation, or feel yourself
sinking into it, these suggestions may help:

•Remember there is no single "right" way to do this.
Trying to exactly mimic what another person has done

135

probably isn't going to work. Each case is unique because the personalities and problems in each case are unique.

•If you don't take care of yourself — take time to eat, sleep, catch your breath, and pray — you will burn out quickly and be of little use to anyone, including yourself. The situation in which you find yourself is not a sprint, it's a marathon. Yes, someday it will end but that may be a long, long time from now. In the meantime, if you do not pace yourself, sometimes even pamper yourself, you won't be able to keep going. That's not because you're weak, it's because you're human.

•The big picture can look and feel overwhelming. Sometimes it helps to break it down into the many tiny pieces that make up the whole. What you have to do for your parent. Your children. Your spouse. Your job. Yourself. The lists may be long but somehow no single item is overpowering.

•Prioritize your tasks. Making those lists helps. Obviously, getting Mom to her doctor's appointment is more important than vacuuming her apartment.

•Give away some of the low-priority duties. Someone else can be hired to do the apartment cleaning. Someone else — the bakery department at the local grocery store — can supply the brownies you're supposed to send to the next Cub Scout den meeting.

•Get support for yourself. Groups for caregivers and organizations that focus on your parent's particular illness or condition can help you deal with what you are facing. Doctors, social workers, and the Area Agency on Aging can give you local contacts. *(See chapter 47 on finding help and "Resources" in the back of the book.)*

•Write it down. Dates and schedules and all that information from doctors, therapists, pharmacists, teachers, coaches, your boss, your spouse, your kids. . . . There's no way a person can remember all the things you need to remember.

It may seem the day is completely packed, but if you jot down your own "to do" list, you may discover there's half an hour free here. Twenty minutes there. A little oasis that gives you something to look forward to. A short break to at least partially recharge your batteries before you have to go, go, go again.

Stay with me, Lord, when I feel like I'm going to blow my stack. Please hurry up and give me more patience. And Mom, too.

60. Anger

At times, anger can be a dominant emotion in the aging parent-adult child relationship for many reasons. Reasons that would be easier to identify and understand if both people weren't already so drained, both physically and emotionally.

From your mother's point of view, there have been so many changes, so many losses, that her life seems out of control. Other people, the cold, hard facts of aging, and nature continue to chip away at what she can do. At who she is. If she does admit she needs some extra help in a particular area, the cost for that help may seem outrageous, and as she's done for so many years, she continues to save diligently for her "old age."

Dad may feel angry because he thinks you owe him something in return for all his years of parenting and he may not think he's getting a fair shake. And, at the same time, he may feel resentment — the perfect breeding ground for anger — that your roles as parent and child are reversing.

From your point of view, you're angry at what's happening to your mother or father whose health continues to deteriorate. You want to reverse it, or at least stop it, but you can't. You don't want to become the "parent." You may, at times, want to ignore the whole situation.

You might be mad at Dad for getting old. Mad at Mom for fighting you when you try to help. Mad at health-care professionals who may be doing their job all right but don't seem to understand that this is *your* parent and that makes it different. Mad at your siblings who seem to be doing nothing or doing the wrong things. Mad at God when you can't see what the point to all this is and you lay the blame on him.

Perhaps, after helping your parent, you come home and your spouse and children express resentment that you're spending so much time with Grandma or Grandpa and you just don't have any energy left. You've used up all your patience. At work, at home, and out in public, the slightest problem makes you clench your teeth and seethe.

Identifying why you and your parent have these feelings can be an important first step. It may also help you as a caregiver if you:

•Remember Mom or Dad is not necessarily mad at you. You may simply be the target because you're there or because you make her or make him face all those fears head on.

•Try to find some time for yourself. Look for a support group or good friend where you can "dump" some of that anger.

•Forgive yourself.

•Keep in mind that, just as in your relationship with your spouse and children, getting angry with your parent doesn't mean you don't love him or her.

•Go back and apologize. Don't let guilt over anger eat you up. You can start again.

Dear God, I'm sorry for the things I've done wrong. Help me see what I've done right.

61. Guilt

The problem with guilt is that sometimes we deserve it. And we know it. We can't cast the first stone. We make mistakes, we hurt people, we're lazy or arrogant or selfish and we feel bad about it.

And rightly so.

Guilt — that pang of conscience, that ache of remorse — can goad us into being better people. In the same way that a body uses pain to signal an injury that needs attending, the conscience can send a message of guilt that forces us to examine our actions; guilt forces us to consider what we have done and what we have failed to do.

All too frequently for the adult child caring for an aging parent, the guilt alarm never stops ringing. The examination of conscience becomes perpetual. The feelings of frustration and inadequacy and doubt never cease.

Sometimes it helps to realize that no matter what you do — no matter how much or how little — the guilt is likely to be there.

•You feel guilty because you don't stop in and see Mom every day. Or you feel guilty because you're spending too much time helping her and think you're neglecting your spouse and kids.

•You feel guilty because you don't live closer to Dad now that he needs extra help. Or you feel guilty because you're the sibling who does live close by and you're resentful — even jealous — that the others don't know the day-to-day hassles you face.

•You feel guilty that Mom gets out of bed and walks to the living room when your sister visits her but she refuses to do that for you. You must be pampering her. Doing too much. Or you feel guilty that she isn't doing well right now. You must be pushing her too hard.

•You feel guilty that sometimes you get mad at Dad because he won't listen to your suggestions. Or you feel guilty that you're not more involved in helping him decide what to do and helping him get it done.

•You feel guilty because Mom wasn't very good at being a parent and you love her but sometimes you just don't like her. Or you feel guilty because she was a super parent and now she needs your help and you're not coming through for her the way she did for you.

•You feel guilty because you've been a pretty good son or daughter all your life but now, when Dad is really relying on you, you're just not making it. Or you feel guilty because you were pretty wild when you were younger and you didn't listen to him and you know that hurt him.

•You feel guilty that you didn't go into nursing or some other career that would really benefit Mom now. Or you feel guilty that you can help all kinds of people at work — strangers, really — but Mom just drives you up the wall.

•You feel guilty about feeling guilty all the time. Or you feel guilty for giving yourself a break and not feeling guilty.

•And maybe hardest of all, you feel guilty because sometimes you imagine what a relief it will be when Dad has died. And then you can't believe you feel this way.

As if your emotions aren't already stirred up, overworked, and muddled enough, your parents, siblings, spouse, and kids might not be blameless.

Mom or Dad knows what buttons to push — the phrase, the gesture, the sigh, the stare — to make you feel guilty, make you feel like a little kid.

Brothers and sisters likewise haven't forgotten their sibling's emotional weak spots, and at times, they're not above exploiting that knowledge.

A spouse can pour on guilt.

Children — even little ones — can be masters at using guilt to manipulate their parents.

And society is not shy about showing its disapproval. It would have you believe all the elderly are poor, lonely, forgotten people because of an adult child's selfishness. And likewise, it claims, placing a loved one in a nursing home — or even considering such a move — is always cruel and immoral.

While your head may realize these things aren't so, sometimes your heart believes them.

The truth is, even after a parent dies, the guilt can live on.

"I should have. . . ."

"I shouldn't have. . . ."

"Why did I. . . ?"

"Why didn't I. . .?"

Guilt can easily become a constant companion, and if left unchecked, if allowed to race freely, it continuously feeds the twin fires of exhaustion and anger.

These, then, are some strategies to help keep guilt under control:

•Remember that you are a human being. Like all humans, you are not perfect. Not a perfect spouse. Not a perfect parent. Not a perfect son or daughter. Not perfect at work or home or anywhere else. You will never be a perfect caregiver.

Never.

•Remember you don't have to do everything for an aging parent.

It is not required that you meet all Dad's needs yourself. Give away some of the work. If there isn't enough time to clean his house and make all his meals or if you can't bring yourself to give Dad a bath, there are very competent, qualified people who can do those things. People in social service jobs who provide home and personal care.

Instead, use your time and energy to do those things with him that you really want to do. The things that mean the most to you and to him. The ones that will mean the most to you after he is gone.

Who ever heard of a grieving child saying, "No, I didn't get to talk much to Dad near the end but I'm just so thankful I kept his kitchen floor spotless"?

You are not in this alone. Ask for help from siblings, fellow parishioners, friends, neighbors, the community, and social service professionals. Many people would like to help but really don't know what you need and so they offer a vague "Just let me know what I can do." Believe them. Let them know specifically what they can do.

"I need to get these items at the grocery store."

"I just don't have time to get all of the yard work done."

"I need someone to just be with Mom for a couple of hours this Thursday afternoon."

•Remember you can set limits. As Mom's health continues to fail, she's going to need more and more attention, but that does not mean you will be able to continue to match that need. Permit yourself to say, "I can't do that."

•Remember that sooner is better than later. Don't wait for a crisis to arise before getting supplemental help. Don't wait until you are at — or are near — burnout.

•Remember that there are others who are facing the same insurmountable challenges you are. Support groups are available with members who will listen and understand.

•Finally, remember you must accept the fact that no matter how much you do for an aging parent, no matter how well you do it, a parent's health is going to deteriorate. A parent is going to die. This isn't a reflection on you and the quality of care you provide. It's a fact of human nature.

And it's not your fault.

*Thank you, heavenly Father, for the friends and
co-workers who understand.*

62. Words That Sting, Words That Comfort

If your parent is seriously ill, you may soon discover the reactions of others, and your own emotions, take surprising twists and turns.

While it may be hard to think about or even to admit to yourself what is happening to your parent, it may be worse yet to have to say those words out loud.

"Mom has had a stroke. . . ."

"Dad was diagnosed with cancer. . . ."

"It's at the stage where nothing else can be done. . . ."

"The doctor says it's only a matter of months. . . ."

Of weeks. Of days.

If your parent is seriously ill, it often means work has to be missed and an explanation needs to be given. It means the normal car-pool arrangement with the neighbor's kids has to be modified. And so on. It means, time and again, those very words — or vague ones that convey the same awful message — need to be repeated.

That's when questions from some fellow members of the middle generation may hurt. When their words seem to imply, "Yes, your parent. But never mine. And here's why."

"How old is your dad?"

"Did your mom smoke?"

"Had he been sick a while?"

"Did she take good care of herself?"

And though it's never explicitly said, the meaning seems clear: Thank God it's your parent who's sick and not mine. Mine is younger. Mine never smoked. Mine is healthy. Mine exercises and eats right.

These people don't mean to be rude or cold, but sometimes their words sting. Theirs is a natural reaction, not unlike what combat veterans recall feeling when they learned a comrade had been killed in battle. There was a sense of relief. A gratefulness that, for now anyway, they have been spared.

Don't be surprised when you feel a strange burst of resentment, or anger, toward members of the older generation who are still healthy. A burst of envy toward your peers whose parents are still strong and vibrant.

Not that you wish them ill. Not that you wish anyone ill. But why are some seniors up and around and doing so well when your aging parent is failing so rapidly?

And how can everyone else behave so normally, continue with business as usual, when your mother, when your father, is so close to death?

There is no easy way of letting go, no gentle way of saying good-bye to a parent. Not even when our faith tells us — that faith which, in many instances, our parents nurtured within us — that death is not the end. That death brings eternal life. Even then, there is no truly satisfying answer to "why my parent?" To "why now?"

It's at this point that the reaction from other members of the middle generation can be incredibly supportive. Frequently, these are people whose parent or loved one has been ill. Whose parent or loved one has died. They know, they understand, they have felt, what you're going through.

Maybe their strength comes from surviving those thoughtless, stinging questions or from walking in the valley of the shadow of death and discovering the Shepherd really is there. These friends and co-workers can offer an unmatched sense of compassion. They can share an amazing grace.

They clearly know the power of the simple "I'm so sorry to hear that. I'll keep you and your parent and your family in my prayers."

Dear God, I'm so tired. I'm so very tired. Sometimes I don't know what to do. I don't know how I can keep on going. I don't know how I can stop.

63. Exhaustion: Care for the Caregiver

Exhaustion is more than just being tired. It's being tired for weeks, being tired for months.

The people around you can't help but notice if you're exhausted, or if you're rapidly — and steadily — approaching exhaustion. It's not unusual for them to comment on it.

The typical response from the exhausted caregiver is to deny it. Why? Because if you admit the problem, you may be expected to somehow change your behavior. To do something about it. Change seems impossible. And you don't want to do anything that would jeopardize your role as caregiver. You really want to continue to be there for Mom or Dad.

At the same time, exhaustion can bring on a sense of helplessness, a sense of hopelessness. The seemingly awful thought that, "I wish all this were over."

The symptoms of exhaustion aren't difficult to spot. They include:

•a feeling of extreme fatigue (even when you do get the chance to sleep, it isn't a restful sleep);

•becoming more emotional, for example, you get angry more quickly and are less patient which increases the risk of abuse and you feel a deep sadness which may lead to depression. *(See chapter 40 on depression)*;

•arguing more with your spouse, your children, your siblings, even with your parent;

•a change in your eating habits (eating all the time or not enough);

•a haggard appearance;

•showing poor judgment;

•having trouble remembering things;

•constantly feeling overloaded and stressed;

•feeling in danger of "crashing," a fear of breaking down and then not being able to care for your parent, or yourself.

What can you do, especially at a time when you feel you're

already doing way too much? These are some suggestions:

•Take a small step back and realize being exhausted isn't good for you personally or for you as a caregiver. An exhausted caregiver can't be a good caregiver. Also, your parent may be able to see your exhaustion and worry about what he or she is doing to you. *(See chapter 11 on being a burden.)*

•Give yourself a tiny break. A minute or two. Go into the bathroom and shut the door or walk out onto the porch. Just a moment to wash your face with cool water or take a few deep breaths. Taking a day off may seem impossible, but you can take a one-minute break. And you can build on that. More breaks, longer breaks. It takes time to go from exhausted to well. Start planning what you'll do. Something to look forward to. Take ten minutes while Dad is watching the news; take fifteen while Mom is napping.

•Get help. *(See chapter 47 on finding help and "Resources" in the back of the book.)* If you have a sibling who lives a distance, this would be a good time to ask him or her to come home for a week or two and give you a break. Not that you would go away on a vacation, just be able to take some time off as the front-line caregiver. (This is assuming your parent isn't critically ill, just heavily dependent on you. This is the time to take a break. You'll want to be with Mom or Dad when his or her condition does become critical.)

•Also, look into respite care. *(See chapter 64 on respite care.)* Even a few hours once a week can help.

•Try to get some exercise. A daily walk around the block will make a difference.

•Remember, it's better — and easier — to prevent exhaustion than to reach that point and have to come back from it. You're not being selfish if you take breaks, get some exercise, eat right, get your sleep, and ask for help.

•Consider joining a caregivers' support group. Many caregivers find this extremely beneficial.

•Admit the best way to be a good caregiver, to be good to your parent, is to be good to yourself. If you continue to take care of yourself, you can continue to provide the first-rate, loving, compassionate care you want your parent to have.

> *Lord, help us figure out a way Dad and I*
> *can each have a break.*

64. Respite Care

Human beings weren't created to work nonstop seven days a week, fifty-two weeks a year. Our bodies and our minds simply can't maintain that grueling schedule. But in many ways, this is exactly what many primary caregivers try to do. And it's not good for them or for the people in their care.

"Respite care" is a term that's becoming more common. It means a break for someone who is taking care of an ill person, a rest for the person primarily responsible for the well-being of another. In some instances, it's a mother taking care of her severely disabled child; in others, it's an adult child and a sick parent. In still others, it's one aging parent taking care of his or her ill spouse.

No matter what the particular circumstances may be, the basic truth is the same: A primary caregiver needs to take breaks or soon will burn out, soon will be unable to take care of anyone, including himself or herself.

These are some points to consider:

•Caregiving is a complicated experience. It's physically and emotionally draining. There's a tremendous sense of responsibility coupled with strong feelings of guilt: I'm not doing enough. I'm not doing this well. Sometimes I don't want to do this and I wish someone else would.

Without a break, without some type of respite care, anger may surface, and with it an increased risk of physical and verbal abuse which should not be tolerated. If abuse is happening already, it's a clear indication respite care is not only needed, but overdue.

•Respite care does not mean a week off every six months or a free weekend every few months (although those types of breaks are also very helpful and healthy). It's several hours, perhaps once or twice a week, away from the situation with someone else assuming the role of caregiver.

But often that's more easily said than done. It can be hard for you, a primary caregiver, to allow someone else to do your job, even for a short while. Then, too, others — including family members — may not understand why you need to get away. The person in your care may not understand either. He or she may add to your guilt by apologizing for being such a "burden."

•Don't be surprised if you do feel guilty when you're taking a break. If you blame yourself because you need to get away for a time. If you feel bad because in some ways you might not want to go back.

You need to remember that respite care will help you be a better caregiver. Taking that short step back from the immediate situation will help you see it better. It will give you a moment to catch your breath.

•Remember, too, that the break is for you. Don't fill the time running errands for the person in your care, going grocery shopping, getting the car fixed, and so on. Do something for you.

Have lunch with a friend. Check out a support group for others facing the same situation you are. Go bowling. Play a round of golf. See a movie. Visit the library. Sit in a coffee shop and read the newspaper. Do what you used to like to do but no longer have time for.

•To find someone to help you with respite care, check with the local Catholic social service agency. Ask at the parish. Call "Senior Information and Assistance." *(See chapter 47 on finding help and "Resources" in the back of the book.)*

And keep in mind that in many places, state money is available to cover the cost of respite care *even for people who are not low-income families.*

One final point. Perhaps you are not a primary caregiver but your spouse or parent is. Remember, it may be very difficult for people in that position to say, "I need some time off." They may need a push from you to begin to take those vital breaks. Be gentle, be loving, but be firm as you help them see what a difference respite care can make.

Holy Spirit, help me find someone who will listen without judging. Someone who will understand.

65. The Need to Talk

It doesn't feel like "us" and "them." It feels like "me" and "everyone else." When you're taking care of an aging parent, you may think no one else in the world understands what you're going through.

And to a certain extent, you're right.

No one else in the world has the same combination as you and your parent. Illness or disability. Ages. Locations. Living situations. Family history. Siblings. Emotional, psychological and spiritual strengths and weaknesses. There are an infinite number of variables.

No wonder it's easy to assume that no one else can even come close to comprehending what you're going through. No one else can really help you.

Fortunately, that isn't true.

No matter where you are on the very broad spectrum of "adult child taking care of an aging parent," there is a basic human need to talk about what is happening to you.

To tell someone what your questions are. Your concerns. Your fears.

To say out loud, to give words to, the confusing and overwhelming mix of emotions that fills your mind and your heart.

The temptation is to remain silent. To try to tough it out. But then that inner turmoil will only get worse.

The excuse may be "our family just doesn't do that." As if going for emotional help is a sign of weakness. An admission of failure. It isn't. It's the same as seeking medical attention for a physical problem. If you had appendicitis, would you simply "tough it out"?

But where can you go? To whom can you talk?

•A good first step is to get current and accurate information on the particular condition your parent has. Doctors, nurses, and social workers can give you that information along with suggestions for resources available in the community. This not only gives you the facts you need, but puts you in touch with others who are in similar circumstances.

For some adult children the best choice is to meet with a professional counselor in the field of aging. This person will not tell you what to do. He or she will not supply "the answer." Rather, a counselor is there to help you find the most workable solution. He or she can help you identify and label some of the feelings you're having and explain how typical, and normal, these emotions are for a person going through all the things you are.

• Consider a professionally-run support group. This is a good place to "dump" your feelings without listeners jumping in with solutions or judgments. Sometimes it's easier to "unload" when surrounded by concerned strangers rather than family and friends.

A group like this also offers a feeling of support from the sharing that takes place. And you can learn from other people's experiences. This may *not* be a good choice if you cannot set aside your caregiver role and begin to pick up on and worry about their problems. This doesn't help them or you.

•And a third possibility is finding a friend who will listen to you. This needs to be someone to whom you can say, "I don't want answers, advice or solutions. I just need to talk."

Some individuals, however well-intentioned, can't help offering advice. This doesn't mean they aren't good people or good friends. They just aren't the right ones to meet your needs in this area.

A good way of telling if this is the right person is the way you feel after you've talked to him or her. You shouldn't feel worse. The point is to help you release some of the pent-up emotions churning inside you, not add more to them.

The right friend for this task is one who gives a feeling of taking care of you, of emotionally if not physically putting an arm around you and holding you.

You need a friend who lets you talk, because that's what you really need to do if you are an adult child concerned about an aging parent.

Lord, help Mom and me get on the same wavelength.
We need to talk.

66. Roadblocks to Communication

The television is blaring. Here you went to all the trouble to get off work a little early so you could stop by and see your father, and now he won't even turn down the TV.

He stares at the screen and ignores your attempts at conversation or answers with a curt "uh huh" or "huh uh." Finally, to your amazement and confusion, he gives you a disgusted look, gets up and storms out of the room.

What's the point? you wonder. What's going on here?

A lot. With spoken communication between any two people there's a lot that goes on. And a lot that can go wrong.

First, Dad must be able to hear. The physical mechanics have to work correctly or he's not going to catch all that you're saying.

Second, his brain has to be able to understand and interpret those sounds we call words. This is known as receptive language.

Third, he needs to be able to use expressive language. He has to be able to call up the words he needs to use when he needs to use them.

And fourth, the physical mechanics also have to be working properly for him to correctly speak those words in an intelligible manner.

Hearing loss, memory loss, or a stroke are only some of the malfunctions that can make it difficult to converse with your parent. Identifying where the problems are is the first step toward compensating for those roadblocks that may be the source of Mom or Dad's fear, frustration, anger, isolation and paranoia.

Sometimes it's very clear after a person has had a stroke that her ability to converse has been severely impaired. However, if she's experiencing a gradual loss of hearing — a common occurrence among the elderly — then the problem may go unnoticed or unacknowledged by her and other family members. *(See chapter 32 on hearing.)*

These are suggestions to help you more easily talk with your parent:

•Be sure to face Dad when you're talking to him. Speak slowly. It may take him a little longer to come up with the right word. Don't jump in and finish his sentences for him.

•If Mom has a problem with complicated questions ("What did you have for breakfast today?"), substitute a series that can be answered with "yes" or "no." ("Did you eat breakfast today? Did you have toast? Did you have fruit?")

•In a group setting, have one family member be the "summarizer." This person sits next to Dad and tells him what's being said, but not word for word. ("Karen is talking about her new car.") Take turns serving as the summarizer so the older person won't come to depend on only one family member who may not make it to all gatherings.

•Try to be patient. Remember, even in a world of microwave meals, instant replays, and buzzing fax machines, some things still can't be rushed. Conversing with your parent can give you a much needed opportunity to slow down, take a deep breath and remember, once again, what's really important in life.

Lord, it really is a tangled web we can weave. . . . Don't let me make that mistake.

67. Keeping Secrets, Telling Lies

It's a bad idea to keep secrets from immediate family members if your mother or father is facing a terminal illness. Not always telling Mom or Dad the truth — the whole truth — is a mistake, too.

Sooner or later, that secret, the whole truth, is going to be revealed. When that happens, a loving relationship based on trust is damaged. People are hurt more than they would have been if everyone had simply been honest from the beginning.

But it's *so* tempting.

If Dad is terribly frightened by the words "cancer" and "malignant," why not gloss over what the doctor has said? Why not just refer to his condition as "stomach problems" and keep his spirits up by telling him he'll soon be back on his feet and good as new?

Why not? Because he's an adult. Because he has the right to hear the truth, even if it's a harsh truth. Unless there are extenuating circumstances — significant dementia, for example — Dad has the right to make his own decisions, and in order to make the best ones possible, he needs to know all the facts.

While it's not unusual — and it's certainly understandable — that an adult child would want to shield a parent, want to protect him or her from as much worry as possible, doing so is also selling a parent short. It may help you to keep in mind that Mom didn't reach old age without going through hard times. She didn't get there without having squarely faced difficulties that couldn't be avoided.

Often a parent, even one who is frail, is much tougher and wiser than an adult child realizes.

If both your parents are still living, there may be times when one of them says to you, "Don't tell your mother" or "Don't tell your father." But a spouse knows when there's a serious problem, and hearing "everything's fine" can make him or her worry even more because obviously everything *isn't* fine. Obviously something is very wrong.

And so your parents share the secret but neither says a word about it. Neither brings up the subject.

The same thing can happen between generations.

Mom is trying to protect you; you're trying to protect her. Neither of you talks about the illness.

Neither says, "This is very hard."

Neither says, "I will miss you."

Neither takes advantage of the fleeting time — the years, the months, the days, that are left.

There may also be times when a parent wants to keep the secret with only one child. "Don't tell your brother. He has enough to worry about with his job." "Don't tell your sister. It will only upset her."

Of course it will add to his worry! Of course it will upset her!

Some things in life are very worrisome, are very upsetting, but worse still is being excluded from an inner family circle.

Why wasn't I told? Did Dad like my sibling more than he liked me? Did Mom have such a low opinion of my ability to cope? Was it my sibling who shut me out?

Keeping such a serious secret — a life-and-death secret — robs a person of the time to prepare for what's going to happen. Time to come to terms mentally, emotionally, and spiritually with the idea that a mother or father is going to die. To come to terms with the idea that I, an aging parent, am going to die.

You need to keep in mind that getting the secret out into the open means more than simply stating it out loud. It means being there for your parents and your siblings as they too acknowledge the harsh reality that must be faced.

It means supporting, encouraging, consoling, and loving one another. It means all of you coming together, one final time, as a family.

But what about not telling the truth when it's *not* a life-and-death situation? Lying seems like such a good idea. The perfect solution.

For example, Mom has made it clear she will not pay for extra medical help at home. If her health insurance doesn't cover a visiting nurse, then she will do without. But you're the one handling her bills now. You know she has plenty of money. She's just being silly. She's just being stubborn. So you go ahead and hire a nurse and tell Mom the insurance company has a new policy. No harm done.

That's not so. When you start lying to your parent or begin withholding information from him or her, harm *is* being done.

When the truth comes out, and it always seems to at the worst possible moment, it may be a long time before trust is reestablished.

"Why didn't you tell me?" is the natural question.

"What else have you been lying about?" comes next.

"What else are you going to lie about?" follows.

You may truly have your parent's best interest at heart. You don't want to upset Dad. You don't want Mom to know because she won't agree with the decision.

But, again, it comes down to this: Your parent has a right to know. Mom needs to know if she is going to make informed choices. Dad needs to know if he is going to be able to prepare for what's coming.

If you're tempted to lie, imagine someone keeping similar, personal, vital information from you. Imagine someone lying to you about it just so you won't worry.

You would be furious. And rightly so.

Imagine hearing that you need a very serious operation next week and that your loved ones, those closest to you, knew for a month, six months, even a year, that this was a possibility.

Yes, you would have been scared for a year. Yes, you would have worried. But you would also have had time to prepare yourself for this. To turn to those loved ones for support.

How can you turn to them now when they didn't even respect you enough to tell you the truth?

And, once again, remember that telling the truth brings an obligation with it. It isn't just a matter of getting those hard words out. It isn't just admitting the reality that exists. It's helping your parent understand what those words mean.

Helping your parent get whatever additional information is needed.

Helping your parent cope with new and perhaps horrible knowledge. Come to grips with that grim reality.

Telling the truth is another way you show your love for your parent.

Love between adults makes many demands, and one of them is honesty. Love never tricks a person. Love never uses a person's resources without that person's knowledge. Love never says "I know what's best for you and so you have no say in this."

The truth can be cold and cruel and terrifying. When we tell that truth or when we hear it, we need the warmth, the caring, and the comfort only a loved one can give.

Thank you, heavenly Father, for my brothers and sisters.
Help us work together to make Dad's life better.

68. Family Roles and Relationships

As a child you probably didn't like it when others compared you to your siblings. Now, as an adult caring for an aging parent, those similarities and differences can continue to influence the challenges your family is facing.

It can help to remember that you and your siblings each have a unique relationship with your parent. You've each played particular roles in the family. Those roles have been shaped, in part, by your personalities. At the same time, those roles helped shape your personalities.

You each have unique abilities, life experiences, and training. You each have your own way of handling things. Your own strengths and weaknesses. It's a small wonder then that when it comes to helping your mother or father, there may at times be some differences of opinion, some friction.

These are some points to consider about dealing with — or, better still, avoiding — sibling conflict:

•Certainly the best way to handle this is to sit down with your siblings and talk about these things before there's a medical crisis or a personality clash. To list the "what ifs" and come up with workable solutions. Even without this kind of gathering or conference call, if you are or are going to be the primary caregiver, it may help if you jot down a likely "what if" list.

•Even if your parent already needs help, maybe the siblings just can't be in the same room with each other without arguments erupting. There may be a lot of family dynamics going on here: anger, resentment, disagreements over money, a history of abuse, alcoholism, and so on. If that's the case, ask a geriatric social worker to be there to facilitate the meeting. This may be a time when it's necessary to set aside differences — call a temporary cease-fire — and deal with taking care of a parent.

•Perhaps only you and one or two of your siblings meet. The point is to offer the opportunity to everyone.

•At that gathering or during a conference call, make sure everyone has a chance to ask questions and explain concerns. Assignments can be made: staying in touch with the doctor, handling finances, seeing to it that home care is provided and all the rest. Schedules can be set up: Who's driving Dad to the doctor when? Who's going to be with Mom on what days? (Or, for out-of-town siblings, who's going to call her when?)

•Out-of-towners (long-distance caregivers) and those who live nearby are going to have different perspectives. *(See chapters 71 and 72 on long-distance caregiving.)*

A visit home can give a long-distance sibling a chance to offer the primary caregiver a break. And the local sibling should make sure the long-distance brother or sister has some time alone with Mom or Dad.

•It's possible for your parent to give durable power of attorney in different areas to different children. For example, you may have it for medical issues. Your sibling for finances.

•If you are the primary caregiver, don't be shy about asking your siblings for help. They may not know what to do or be intimidated because you seem to be doing everything so well. Sometimes it helps to offer a couple choices: "Can you take Mom to the doctor's on Tuesday afternoon or stay with her Saturday morning?" And when they help, remember how they perform a task might not be how you do it, but both ways may be right.

•There can be incredible strength and comfort in numbers. Common concern for Mom or Dad doesn't have to splinter a family; it can bring members closer together.

*Father, Son, and Spirit, bless my marriage. Thank you for
the love we share.*

69. When You're Married to the Caregiver

If you're the husband or wife of an adult child who is taking
care of an aging parent, it may seem that no matter what you say or
do, it's the wrong thing.

Suddenly you may find yourself an outsider as the immediate
family circle closes ranks.

You may feel tremendously frustrated about your powerlessness:
You cannot make everything all right; you cannot stop the pain your
spouse is feeling.

Here are a few points to consider, a few suggestions, that may
make this time easier:

•Remember that the relationship you have with your in-laws is not
the same as the one your husband or wife has. This is simply human
nature. No matter how close you may have become to your mother- or
father-in-law, your experience is not the same as your spouse's.

So while you may feel the two of you are doing more than
enough to help, your spouse may not feel that way at all.

•Understand that every immediate family has its own little
quirks — good and bad. Maybe Dad has always had a short fuse.
Maybe Mom has never been able to relax if there was one speck of
dust on one stick of furniture.

Maybe family members never talk to one another, they yell.
Maybe they never yell . . . or talk. Whatever the characteristics, they
may intensify under the present, stressful circumstances.

•Don't take it personally if you are suddenly outside the loop. If no
one really wants to hear your opinion because this is a "family" matter.

At the same time, you may very well be affected by the
decisions being made by your spouse and the other siblings. It's not
uncommon that several sons will decide what's best for Mom or Dad
but it is the daughters-in-law who end up providing almost all of the
care. *(See chapter 70 on caring for an in-law or stepparent.)*

Then, too, the opposite may occur. Your spouse's siblings are no help and so it is up to your spouse and you to do everything.

•Know that sometimes you will be the target of your spouse's emotions. The anger, the fear, the sadness, the frustration, the guilt. Again, try not to take it personally. Most likely it's not really meant for you but for something else. For the disease or medical problem that is taking the life of your spouse's parent. For the pain. For death.

•Remember that while it may seem this situation has been going on forever and it will never end, it *is* temporary. It *will* end.

In the meantime, you may feel somewhat neglected, but remember, your spouse is being pulled in many different directions: aging parent, you, the children, the job. This is a time when he or she especially needs your help and your understanding.

A spouse also needs to hear "You're doing a good job helping your parent but *you can't do everything*." It's hard to hear that. It has to be said gently over and over again.

It may seem pretty obvious to you that your spouse has assumed a new role: caregiver to an aging parent. What you need to remember is that during this time, you, too, have a new, special and vital role as well: Taking care of the caregiver. Supporting the caregiver. Consoling the caregiver. Loving the caregiver.

*Lord, bless this family. Even the members I sometimes
don't feel very close to.*

70. Caring for an In-law or Stepparent

Being the caregiver of an in-law can be a lot different from taking care of your own parent.

The same can be true when taking care of a stepparent, if he or she is someone who joined the family after you reached adulthood or there has always been friction between you.

Every newlywed soon learns that you don't marry an individual, you marry a family — a family that may be very different from your own family of origin. What many newlyweds may not realize is that promising to stick by one another "in sickness and in health" can include a family member's sickness, too.

Being an in-law's caregiver is a task that's both easier and at the same time harder.

It's easier because you probably don't know your mother- or father-in-law as well as you know your own parent and the "caregiver-patient" role may feel less awkward. You have no memories of being cared for by him or her. And then, too, your in-law probably isn't able to "push your buttons" the way your family members can.

As you well know, taking care of a parent can be a highly emotional time. But with an in-law, it's sometimes easier to feel one step removed. This doesn't mean you aren't concerned or that you don't provide compassionate, loving care, but — no matter how close you are to your in-law — it's just not the same as taking care of your own mother or father.

On the other hand, it may be more difficult because you may feel you've been forced into this role. It's not uncommon for a son to want to take care of a parent, but in reality, it's the daughter-in-law who provides the care.

You may have little interest in taking care of an elderly person. You may not even want to. Especially someone who, if you and your in-law live a distance apart, is pretty much a stranger.

But whether you and your in-law have always been close or haven't seen much of each other over the years, your relationship shifts once you begin your new role. Less parent to adult child or friend to friend, it naturally becomes more caregiver to patient. And, in doing that, you can't help but invade your in-law's privacy.

Now you see your mother-in-law disrobed and need to help her with a bath. Now you know your father-in-law's financial situation.

There can be feelings of jealousy. You would rather be doing this for your own parent or would rather have done it when your own parent needed it. Instead, you're putting so much of your time and energy, so much of yourself, into helping your spouse's parent.

These are some suggestions:

•From the very beginning, involve your spouse as much as possible. What you're doing is a wonderful gift to your spouse, but it's also something that can be extremely hard on your relationship. Your spouse may have unrealistic expectations about what you can do. And may — completely unfairly — in some way hold you partially responsible as your in-law's health continues to deteriorate.

•Get your spouse's siblings involved. If they live a distance, maybe they could help with finances (if that's needed) or with keeping extended family members up-to-date on what's happening. And, during visits to their parent, they could offer you some respite time.

•Reserve the right to set limits. You can do this, but you can't do that. Be honest. Also admit when you've reached a point of, or are fast approaching, exhaustion. Don't hesitate to bring in as much outside help as you need even if the family frowns on that because it just "isn't the way we do things."

The way they're doing things may be to step back and let the burden of being primary caregiver fall on your shoulders. No one can carry that load alone.

Dear God, I really hate being so far away from Mom. I know you're always close to her, always watching out for her.

71. Long-distance Caregiving, I: By Phone

"Long-distance caregiver" is a relatively new term used to describe an increasing number of baby boomers who live in one part of the country but are trying to monitor an aging parent's health and well-being in another.

While there's no written job description for the role, most adult children who find themselves in it are quick to mention worry, frustration, guilt and enormous telephone bills.

How do you know if Mom is eating right? Why didn't she tell you she was going in for that test? Why did you take this job so far away? How many voice-mail messages do you have to leave before her doctor calls you back? What's going on there?

The urge is to hop on a plane and go find out. The reality in most cases is commitments to spouse, children, and a job, not to mention the high cost of airfare, make that impossible.

If you must be a long-distance caregiver:

•Make sure your name, address, and phone number are *posted* by your parent's phone with a note asking that you be contacted if there is a problem.

•Be certain your parent's doctor has the same information. The same holds true for any home-care services people (visiting nurse, housekeeper, physical therapist, and so on) who may be working with your mother or father.

•Give your name, address, and phone number to the neighbor or the friend who is already in regular contact with your parent and get his or her number. If your mother lets Mrs. Jones know what's going on, *don't* ask Mrs. Smith to start checking up. Also, let Mrs. Jones know that if you cannot reach your parent, you'll be giving her a call. And ask her if it's all right for you to check in with her once in a while just to see how Mom is doing.

•If your parent is going to be released from a hospital or nursing home, ask to speak to the discharge planner and do so *early*, before the day your parent goes home. This is the staff member who figures out what services your parent needs and how frequently he or she needs them. *(See chapter 29 on being in the hospital.)*

•If you're looking for health or service resources in your parent's area, call telephone information for that area code and ask for "Senior Information and Assistance," or call the toll-free Eldercare Locator number: 1-800-677-1116. Most areas have case management services. Through a state-subsidized or private program, a case manager can coordinate the team of health and home-care professionals who will be working with an elderly person. *(See*

*chapter 47 on finding help, chapter 49 on hiring a case manager
and "Resources" in the back of the book.)*

When you talk to your parent on the phone:

•Pay attention to what Mom is telling you. Is there something
new going on? For example, is she talking about friends dying? Is she
suddenly concerned about a particular ache or pain?

•If both parents are still living, spend time talking to each alone.
Ask Mom how she's doing and ask her how Dad is doing. Ask Dad
the same.

•Call frequently and regularly. Agree on a time that's good for
both of you. Mark it on your calendar so you don't forget. A week
probably passes very quickly for you. That may not be true for your
parent who really looks forward to hearing from you and will worry
about you if you fail to call.

•Suggest that your parent jot down a few notes between calls to
get ready for the next one. You do the same. That way neither of you
will forget something important that needs to be discussed or a bit of
news that will be fun to share.

*Please, God, help me figure out the finances and the
scheduling so I can get back home. And help me be ready
for what I may find there.*

72. Long-distance Caregiving, II: Going Home

As we wrote in the preceding chapter, the telephone can be an
invaluable tool for monitoring your parent's well-being but it works
best when coupled with visits to Mom or Dad.

Those visits — as limited as that time might be — can go a long
way toward meeting the needs of your parent and helping calm your
worries, too. Here are some suggestions for going home:

•Plan ahead. Call Dad's doctor and others working with him

and arrange appointments to meet and discuss how he's doing. Those meetings should include your father. Waiting until you are at Dad's house to begin setting up meetings means trying to make arrangements on short notice and spending time on the phone that could be better spent with him.

•When you do meet, have your list of questions and concerns ready, based on what Mom has said — and not said — during your telephone conversations, on what you have observed during this visit with her, and on the most current assessment. (How have your parent's health and living conditions changed since the last time you were home? What needs have become more prominent? Any new ones?)

•Don't panic at what seems like drastic changes, including a great deal of deterioration. Because you haven't witnessed those changes on a day-by-day or week-by-week basis, the difference between now and six months ago may be more startling to you than to your parent or a sibling who has been around more frequently. Their failure to mention these changes to you does not mean they have been hiding them from you, they simply may not see them. You each have a unique perspective; all are helpful when trying to make an accurate evaluation.

•Charging in with all the answers often means meeting with stiff resistance, not just from Dad but from your siblings who may live closer and also have been playing a role in taking care of him. Ask how you can help and offer suggestions. Work *with* your father and siblings.

•Think *small*. Prioritize those needs. Begin with suggestions that are least threatening and that allow your parent the greatest amount of independence. Maybe this is the visit to set up some sort of housekeeping. The next visit may be the right time to arrange for assistance with finances. But begin the process now by raising the issue with your parent.

•Realize you're not going to fix all the problems in one visit. Give yourself time. Becoming agitated with yourself, your parent, or your siblings only gets in the way.

•Remember that your role as long-distance caregiver is something new not just to you but to our society. In days gone by, most members of the extended family lived close to one another and those who did move far away returned infrequently, if at all. Automobiles, interstate highways, jets, telephones, and a host of other advances that made our world smaller have also made the role of long-distance caregiver possible.

More suggestions and a care-management work sheet are available in an American Association of Retired Persons' booklet. There's no charge. *(See "Resources" in the back of the book.)*

I don't want to say good-bye to Mom, Lord.
I don't want her to go.

73. Going Home to Say Good-bye

It usually begins with a long distance phone call. A brother reaches you at work. A sister leaves a message on your answering machine at the house. Mom is very sick. Dad is dying. Come home. As fast as you can. Now.

Come home to say good-bye.

If you live a distance from your parent, you don't want to think about the day that call will come but you know someday it will.

And, in a way, you may hope it will come because, as terrible as that experience is going to be, it will be worse if the call comes after Mom or Dad dies. If there is no chance, no last chance, to say, "I love you. I want to thank you. I'll miss you."

What can you do to prepare for this time? There's no way to take away the pain, but these are some suggestions that may make this period less confusing:

•If Dad is seriously ill, or his health is steadily declining, think about what needs to be done in order for you to get to him on short notice. Who can cover for you at work? What arrangements need to be made for your spouse and kids?

•Before the time arrives, ask Mom what she would like when her death is near. Each of you may hesitate to bring up the subject because you don't want to upset the other. But maybe your mother would feel much better if she knew for certain she was going to have her blue rosary beads with her. Maybe she doesn't want to offend anyone but she doesn't like hospital room mob scenes and wants the opportunity to see each of her children privately when she's near death.

•Keep in mind a parent's final days are not a good time to rehash — or renew — old arguments or wounds within the family. If you need to resolve something between yourself and a parent or sibling, do it before this, when emotions won't be running so high.

Perhaps you need to resolve a family issue for yourself on your own or with the help of a counselor or therapist. To come to terms with the issue knowing you and other family members are never going to reach agreement, never going to make peace when it comes to this.

•Remember that when an aging parent is dying, all the family members are sad and frightened but each may show it in a different way. Each may need to cope with it in a different way. One may want to be quiet and alone, spending time in the hospital chapel. Another may keep busy handling details that need attending. One may chatter nonstop. Another may always be demanding the latest update on a parent's condition from the medical staff.

Let each person do what works best for him or her. And you do what works best for you.

•And finally, realize that even though people beyond the immediate family aren't feeling the same pain and confusion all of you are feeling, it doesn't mean they don't care. Think back to when a neighbor, a parishioner, or a co-worker's aging parent was dying. It's only natural that your feelings then weren't as intense as they are now when it's your own mom or dad.

Remember people do care. Deeply. They may stumble over the words or hesitate even to say them, but they want to offer their support, their prayers, and their love.

*Heavenly Father, I know this isn't going to be easy for my
children to do. I know it's important that they do it.
Be with us all.*

74. Preparing Your Children to Visit Your Parent

Visiting an elderly grandparent who is frail and ill can be tough
for your children whether they're youngsters or teens. There are
things you can do before that meeting to make the time together less
stressful and more rewarding for both generations.

•First, give your kids the basic information about their
grandparent's condition in words they can understand. For example,
"emphysema" may mean nothing to them. Tell them Grandma may
need to be on oxygen. She might have difficulty talking and may
experience a shortness of breath while they are there.

•Talk about what equipment is being used. For instance, if your
parent is on an IV or has a catheter bag hanging beside the bed.

•Go over appropriate and inappropriate behavior, whether the
visit is taking place in a bedroom, a nursing home, or a hospital.
There's no running around. Like a library or a church, it's a quiet place.

•Warn them that all visitors may need to step out of the room if
Grandpa has to take care of some personal business with a nurse or
attendant.

•If Grandma has dementia, talk about what symptoms the
children might see. Explain how she might not recognize them — or
you — and might speak as if a long-dead relative is still living.

•Remind your children that when they aren't feeling well they
tend to be cranky. The same is true with grown-ups. Grandpa may
seem angry or get upset easily but it's not because he's mad at them.

•Offer some suggestions for what they might talk about with
their grandparent. They can tell what they're doing in school. They
can talk about their sports team or about their pets.

•Suggest that younger children might want to prepare some
homemade gift, maybe a drawing to hang on the wall. Explain to
older ones that their visit is a gift, one that can mean a great deal to
their grandparent.

•Remember that your children may have very few, or no, memories of this person, especially if you live a distance from your parent and, over the years, visiting has been limited. Your father may seem to be only a little old man lying in bed. Tell your kids stories about him. About the Dad you knew. This will help your children understand why it's so important to you that they see him. So important they get to spend time together.

•It might help to dig out the old family photo albums. Let your kids see pictures of Mom when she was young. Celebrating birthdays. Opening Christmas presents. Enjoying a vacation. Help your children understand she has a history. She has lived a long life.

•This may be especially difficult, but just as you talk about how life begins when there's a newborn around, talk about how life ends. How Grandpa is near the end of life on earth and what that means. Why it's important that, just as life is respected when it comes into the world, so it needs to be as it leaves.

•Talk about how precious life is. And how, just because someone is bedridden, just because someone isn't making money, it doesn't mean that person's life has no value. Maybe this is a time for Grandma to pray. Maybe it is a time to reminisce with family and friends and say good-bye. Maybe it is all of those, a time to prepare for the life that comes after this life.

•Remind your children they will be in the presence of history. In the presence of wisdom. Tell them you hope that years from now they will remember this day, this visit — this person who has meant so much to you.

On Death and Dying

Thank you, Jesus, for the people who are helping Dad now that he's nearing the end of his life. Richly reward them for what they do for families like ours.

75. Hospice

Hospice offers tremendous support for both the terminally ill patient and the caregiver.

First established by Dr. Cicely Saunders in Great Britain in 1977, it's a concept that has spread to countless communities. It's one that's endorsed by medical professionals and covered by Medicare and many insurance policies.

Typically, hospice provides service for a person who is terminally ill and has less than six months to live. It uses a team approach, and that team includes the patient, the caregiver, the doctor, nurses, aides, respite volunteers, a social worker, and a spiritual counselor.

It manages the symptoms of the disease or illness (controlling pain, for example) but doesn't offer curative measures.

A patient can receive hospice care in his or her home with the family or caregiver's support or in a hospice setting (which is usually associated with a medical facility). It's designed to help a patient stay in a familiar or at least a more homelike environment. One that offers more personalized, less institutionalized care.

In a hospice setting, a patient has more control over his or her dying. That's not to say this is a form of assisted suicide — which hospice opposes — rather, the patient is actively involved in making decisions. Among these would be what, if any, extraordinary means should be taken to prolong life.

Also, hospice stresses providing the patient with full and accurate information about his or her condition.

With the help of the hospice team, a patient is encouraged to tell his or her life story, and to take the opportunity to explore the meaning of death.

After the patient has died, bereavement counseling is available for the caregiver.

Hospice's goal is to make a person as comfortable as possible at the end of his or her life and to help that person prepare for death.

Information about hospice is available from your parent's doctor, the nearest hospital or the telephone book. *(See "Resources" in the back of the book.)*

There's no doubt hospice has been an incredible experience for many families, but that doesn't mean your parent — or you — should feel obligated to choose it. For some families, hospice simply may not be a good fit. That doesn't mean you aren't "doing this right." "Right" is whatever works best for your parent and you.

But it's good to keep in mind that hospice workers — much to their credit — are known for their ability to help each family develop a plan that does fit its unique situation.

We all make mistakes, Lord. Help Mom deal with the issues that are bothering her.

76. Helping a Dying Parent Find Forgiveness and Peace

An aging parent who is facing death may feel the need to make peace with a friend, with a relative, with a former spouse or with God.

Just as you help your aging parent eat right and get to doctors' appointments, you may also be called on to help Mom or Dad prepare spiritually for death. The task may seem overwhelming for both you and your parent. One for which neither of you feels equipped.

But helping a mother or father find that peace, helping him or her turn or return to God, can make such a difference for both a parent who is dying and a child who is being left behind.

These are suggestions for helping your mom or dad heal old wounds by admitting mistakes, offering apologies, and accepting forgiveness:

•Dad may need the opportunity to talk about serious matters. Matters that weigh heavily on his mind, matters that burden his soul. It's not uncommon for a person facing death to review his life. Some things may need to be said out loud. Getting to that point may depend on your willingness to spend time with your father and your openness to listen to what he has to say.

Sometimes saying something out loud, bringing it out into the open, shows it in a different, a clearer, light. It's easier to see how a mistake could have been made. How a falling out could have happened. How no single person was entirely to blame or entirely without blame. Talking about it openly may make it easier to come to the realization that it's time to forgive others and oneself.

•Your mother may need to get in touch with someone. Often the other party wants to make peace, too. Let Mom know that you can help arrange the chance to talk to one another.

•Maybe the person with whom your dad wants to reconcile won't talk to him. Maybe that person has already died. Suggest your father write a letter to that person, saying all the things he would say if they could sit down face to face. Not that this letter will ever be mailed, but writing it can be a way to say, "Please, forgive me; I forgive you."

•Sometimes a parent feels talking or writing just isn't enough. Mom has to do something more. Maybe it's going to her parents' or spouse's grave and praying, crying, yelling, and apologizing there. Maybe it's compiling a list of regrets and then burning it. Again, letting go. Again, asking and accepting forgiveness.

•Your parent may need to cry a lot. Your parent may need to turn more to prayer. Be open to both.

•If there are big issues that you can't help with, Mom or Dad might benefit from talking with a counselor. Hospice social workers have the skills to help a person sort through a life review.

•Finally, encourage and arrange for Mom or Dad to take advantage of the sacrament of reconciliation — confession — and the anointing of the sick. *(See chapters 54-57 on returning to the Church and the sacraments.)* No matter how long your parent may have been away from the Church, no matter what he or she may have done, an all-loving God is waiting with open arms to offer forgiveness and peace now and, at the time of death, to share his eternal joy.

Dad and I need to get ready for his death, Lord. We can't do that without you.

77. Preparing for Death

Death has been surrounded by folklore and traditions throughout human history. Every culture has rituals and beliefs about preparing for death, about death itself, and about life after death.

What's it *really* like to die? We don't know. Many talk of "near-death" experiences but "nearly dying" and dying aren't the same thing.

Maybe your parent has been near death several times. But having a parent at death's door and saying good-bye to each other are different from having a parent die. There's a finality to death that's like nothing else on earth.

How do you prepare for that moment? How do you help your parent prepare? Here are some suggestions:

•Examine your own feelings and beliefs and let Dad talk about his if he wants to. Maybe the two of you don't see eye-to-eye. One or the other isn't so sure about the idea of heaven and an all-loving God.

If he's afraid, offer him comfort. If you're the one who's uncertain, trust your dad. This isn't the time to have a theological or scientific argument. Help him be at peace with what's happening.

•Prepare by reading up on death and the dying process. What typically happens, step by step.

•Ask where Mom would like to die. At home? At the hospital? Under what conditions? Alone? With family at her bedside? With friends nearby? Ask her more than once because as time goes by and she's closer to death, her answers may change.

•Based on your parent's preferences, try to get a mental picture of what this will be like and what your role will be. If at home, are you leading prayers? Wiping Dad's forehead with a cool washcloth? If at the hospital, are you at his bedside? In the hall? In the chapel?

•Try to take care of necessary funeral details ahead of time so it's easier to focus on the immediate needs of your family. *(See chapter 79 on funerals.)*

•If the two of you haven't settled some issues, don't get into an argument over them. Let them go, knowing you may have to deal with them after your parent has died.

•If Mom asks for a "deathbed promise" — to get along with a sibling, to quit smoking, and so on — agree to give it your best effort (knowing, but again, not getting into an argument about it, that giving it your best effort doesn't mean guaranteeing success).

•Don't wait until the last minute to say "good-bye" to each other. To literally say it or the equivalent. It may be tremendously difficult for family members and a dying loved one to get those words out, but after your parent has died, it can mean a great deal to you and other family members.

•Help Dad prepare spiritually. *(See chapters 53-57 on prayer, returning to the Church and the sacraments.)*

•Realize that, while for obvious reasons this is an extremely difficult time for you, it can also be a very rich time. Up until now you've been given the chance to show, in so many ways, how much you love your mom. Now you're being given the gift of being near, being with, her as she dies. You're being given the opportunity to exchanges good-byes. You're being given the blessing of being there as your responsibility for her care ends and her heavenly Father calls her home.

You'll be there as her heavenly Parent reaches out to gently lead her to eternal peace, to eternal joy, to eternal life.

Help me find the right words, Holy Spirit.
Help me do this right.

78. Talking to Your Children About Death

It's difficult, if not impossible, to explain death in words children will understand when we don't even really understand it ourselves.

Still, it's important to take the time to talk to your children. These are some points to keep in mind:

•It's easier to talk to your children before your parent is near death. Easier to talk about death in general, or the death of someone who isn't too close to the family, than to talk about the death of a loved one. For example, to bring up the subject after an elderly parishioner or neighbor has died.

•It isn't just your parent's approaching death that can be upsetting to your child; it's seeing you so upset. Don't gloss over or hide your feelings, but be aware that your child is picking up on them.

•Your child may take the death of your parent very personally. "I'm not going to see *my* grandma ever again."

•A child's sense of security can be rattled. "If Grandpa can die, that means Dad can die. If Dad can die, that means I can die."

•In some ways, talking to your child about death is like explaining the birds and the bees. You use words and concepts that someone at his or her age level will more easily understand. At the same time, it helps to remember that different children have different strengths and weaknesses. One child is more intellectual. Another more easily frightened. A third, more sensitive. Use an approach that fits each child best. It's also easier to talk one-on-one before bringing up the subject with your children as a group.

•Avoid talking about death as "falling asleep" or using similar analogies. Phrases like those may make it difficult for some children to sleep because they're afraid if they do, they too will die. Also, if they see Grandma napping, they become frightened that she has died. Another common explanation — "God wanted Grandpa with him in heaven" — can make God seem pretty selfish, if not downright mean.

•This can be a good time to talk about spiritual beliefs. About bodies and souls. Yes, we won't see Grandma again here on earth, but where she's going is a much better place. Where she's going she'll be happy forever, and someday we'll all be there, together again.

•Local Catholic book stores have age-appropriate books for children about death. Among the best is *Water Bugs and Dragonflies* by Doris Stickney (The Pilgrim Press, New York).

Holy angels, lead Mom into paradise. Escort her to her loving Father. Welcome her home.

79. Funerals, Memorial Services, and Cremation

Years ago Catholic funeral Masses talked of "wrath" and "mourning" and the priest was robed in black vestments. Now, while acknowledging the sorrow survivors feel, the emphasis is on the "paschal mystery" — Christ's resurrection — and the celebrant wears white. Now funerals speak of eternal life, of "angels leading you into paradise."

These are some points to keep in mind:

•Some people have no problem talking about their own funerals. Others are never able to do that. Let your parent take the lead but offer Mom or Dad the opportunity to share his or her preferences.

A funeral Mass? A memorial Mass? A service only at the funeral home? Open or closed casket? A traditional embalming or a cremation? Burial at what cemetery (if your parent doesn't already have a plot)?

•Mom may find great comfort in planning her own service. This can be a chance for her to offer a final "good-bye" to her friends and family. It can give her the opportunity, with the scriptural readings and songs she chooses, to share what she has come to believe about life, death, and resurrection.

Dad may see taking care of this chore as a way of making his death easier for you and his other loved ones. And, being ever frugal, may even have an eye on the bottom line as he picks out a reasonably-priced casket and headstone.

At the same time, it's important to point out Dad may be choosing the least complicated route (cremation, no service, no burial) just to spare the family from having to go through those ordeals. What he may not realize is that a funeral isn't just for the deceased, but in many ways is also for the survivors. It's an opportunity for family and friends to gather and support one another in their sorrow while remembering their loved one with joy. It can be an important — some say vital — step in the grieving process.

•The local priest can give you up-to-date information on choosing between a funeral Mass and memorial service. On having a Rosary or prayer service the night before the funeral. On the burial of the remains or the scattering of the ashes. On what other details (memorial card and pall bearers, for example) need to be considered.

•*A special note about cremation and why the Church now allows it:* About one hundred years ago the Church officially said cremation was forbidden because it was then seen as an "anti-Christian symbol." It was seen — and sometimes meant — as a slap in the face to those who believe in the resurrection of human bodies at the end of time. (The anti-Catholic position was there was no way God could raise a body from the dead if its remains had been reduced to ashes and scattered to the four winds.)

The ban was loosened in the 1960s, by which time the symbolism had faded. In 1970, cremation was approved of except when, in a particular instance, it's being chosen as an anti-Christian statement or to show contempt for the Church.

Lord, I've reached the end. It's over now.
Thanks for your help.

80. Sorting Out, Moving On, Remembering

It's a strange feeling, to no longer have the role of caregiver. The death of a parent brings with it a lot of grief, but it also brings a sense of relief. Maybe strangest of all, it gives you so much time. So much time now to do . . . what?

This hasn't been easy. You're to be congratulated. Taking care of a parent till he or she dies is a tremendous accomplishment. Take pride in the areas where you did well but don't get down on yourself about things you wished you had done differently.

Don't get caught in the traps of "What if . . ." and "I should have . . ." and "Why didn't I. . . ?"

Now there's a feeling of sorting out. Not just your parent's belongings and necessary paperwork, but your own feelings.

In a sense, you've said good-bye to two people. One was the parent who was ill. It's not as hard to let that person move on to a place where there's no suffering as it is to say good-bye to the other one: the healthy person your parent used to be. Somewhere along the line, as you were taking care of your ill parent, both slipped away.

It's good not to make any major changes at this time. There's no reason to rush through cleaning out your parent's belongings either.

Try to respect your parent's wishes, getting mementos to the friends and relatives Mom or Dad wanted them to go to. Seeing to it that this or that item is donated to the charity your parent requested.

As you're sorting these things out, you may just want to sit for a while, surrounded by, holding close, the items that belonged to your mother or father. In this setting, it may be easier for you to pray for your parent. To pray to your parent.

It's going to take time for you to sort out all the feelings, the emotions, you've experienced as a caregiver and are experiencing as a survivor. And, as time goes by, those emotions will shift. They'll change.

There will come a time — and there's no need to rush this —

when you'll want to move on. You may want to find a way, a personal ritual, to say good-bye. There's no right way of doing this. And not doing it isn't wrong.

Again, moving on takes time. Just as you probably didn't become a full-blown caregiver overnight, you won't instantly move on to your "new" life or return to you pre-caregiver life.

You had to learn how to be a caregiver. Now you have to learn how to rebuild your personal life without that role. The role that dominated your world. Now you can go back to jogging. Can return to gardening. Can attend your child's soccer games.

You can return to the little, ordinary joys that were a part of your life before you became a caregiver. You may find new ways to experience that kind of simple joy. The joy of being alive.

In a sense, your life now has two holes. One is in your heart. You miss your mother or father and no one can replace that person. The other is in your calendar. You have so much time, so much *free* time. That commodity that was so precious and so rare just a little while ago now fills your schedule.

A part of sorting out, a part of moving on, is remembering. Some of those memories might be related to your role as caregiver. A good time, a happy time even, during that difficult period.

Maybe it was when Mom talked about her death and she wasn't afraid. Maybe when Dad made some small joke and you were both so tired it seemed like the funniest line ever said and the two of you laughed until tears streamed down your faces.

Certainly, remembering includes the time before your mother or father was ill. Memories from your childhood. Memories of birthdays and anniversaries. Memories of telling and retelling family stories.

It can help to remember your parent's "words of wisdom," his or her personal creed or philosophy. Maybe Mom or Dad never even put it into words. Just lived it. Maybe it's something you want to think about for a time to help you get through the difficult period following your parent's death. Something, if it's a good fit for you, you want to imitate in some way.

It can also help to remember the times your parent comforted you. Those times when he or she helped you when you were hurting or unsure or restless, when you were discouraged or sad or frightened.

It can help if you sit down, take a deep breath, and smile, remembering — acknowledging — that as a caregiver, you did the same for your mother or father.

And now your parent is at peace.

Appendixes

A. Resources for Support

This list is a very small fraction of what's available throughout the country to help your parent and you. *(See also chapter 47 on finding help.)*

Many organizations associated with a particular disease, condition or service have toll-free telephone numbers. Call toll-free directory assistance (800-555-1212) to ask about a national organization's number. Typically, a national organization can provide the number for a local affiliate as well as general information about the disease, condition or service. **All of the numbers and addresses listed were correct at the time of publication.**

Eldercare Locator Services
112 16th St. N.W., Suite 100
Washington, DC 20036
Nationwide assistance directory: 800-677-1116
Sponsored by the National Association of Area Agencies on Aging, Eldercare gives referrals of local organizations and agencies offering services to the elderly, including **Senior Information and Assistance**. It's easiest if you have your parent's ZIP code, but using the city or county will work, too.

Alzheimer's Association
919 N. Michigan Ave., Suite 1000
Chicago, IL 60611-1676
312-335-8700
Information line: 800-272-3900

American Association of Retired Persons (AARP)
601 E St. N.W.
Washington, DC 20049
202-434-2277
Information line: 800-424-3410

You don't need to be an AARP member to receive its publications. Getting the "Caregiver Resource Kit" is a good first step. Among the publications available is one on money management and one on long-distance caregiving.

American Cancer Society
1599 Clifton Road N.E.
Atlanta, GA 30329
404-320-3333
Information line: 800-227-2345

American Dental Association
 (Division of Communications)
211 E. Chicago Ave.
Chicago, IL 60611
312-440-2593

Referrals to state dental associations offering a number of free or low-cost services for the elderly. Free publications.

American Diabetes Association
1660 Duke St.
Alexandria, VA 22314
703-549-1500
Information line: 800-232-3472

American Heart Association (AHA)
7272 Greenville Ave.
Dallas, TX 75231
214-373-6300
Information line: 800-242-8721

AHA Stroke Connection
7272 Greenville Ave.
Dallas, TX 75231
214-706-1556
Information line: 800-553-6321

American Parkinson Disease Association
1250 Hylan Blvd., Suite 4B
Staten Island, NY 10301
718-981-8001
Information line: 800-223-2732

Arthritis Foundation
1330 W. Peachtree St.
Atlanta, GA 30309
404-872-7100
Information line: 800-283-7800

Catholic Charities, U.S.A.
1731 King St., Suite 200
Alexandria, VA 22314
703-549-1390
Catholic Charities can provide information on local services for
the elderly including home health care, counseling, health clinics,
emergency assistance, shelters, and home-care services.

National Hospice Organization
1901 North Moore St.
Suite 901
Arlington, VA 22209
800-658-8898

Medicare
Automated information service: 800-638-6833

Self-help for Hard of Hearing People, Inc.
7910 Woodmont Ave., Suite 1200
Bethesda, MD 20814
301-657-2248
(TTD) 301-657-2249

Social Security Administration
Office of Public Inquiries
6401 Security Blvd.
Baltimore, MD 21235
410-965-1234
Automated service: 800-772-1213

United States Consumer Product Safety Commission
Washington, DC 20207
800-638-2772
Publishes "Safety for Older Consumers: Home Safety Checklist." Free.

B. Reporting Abuse of the Elderly

If you know or suspect an elderly or disabled person is being abused in some way, Adult Protective Services is the agency to contact. APS is there to protect the most vulnerable among us.

While the work of Child Protective Services is better publicized, its counterpart — Adult Protective Services — is still news to a lot of folks.

The particular regulations APS follows may vary from state to state, but local information may be obtained by calling the Area Agency on Aging in your community. *(See "Resources.")*

The sad fact is that as the elderly population continues to increase, more and more seniors are becoming the victims of violence and greed. It's important for fellow family members, for neighbors and for parishioners to be aware of this, to be able to recognize signs of problems, and to know where and how to report concerns.

First, it must be understood why it may be difficult for an older person to say someone is hurting him or her. The elderly may remain silent, and in fact may even try to sabotage the visit of someone investigating the case, because the primary caregiver could get in trouble.

The older person reasons: If he (or she) is taken away, what will happen to me? As far as I know, there is no one else to help. While the present situation may be bad, that would be far worse.

At the same time, the abuser may be doing his or her

185

best to isolate the older person from family and friends. To not let community agencies provide services. To not let anyone talk directly with the older person but to always act as an intermediary. Isolation is a classic warning sign when an older person is being hurt.

How is that person being hurt? It could be:

Physical, mental, emotional, or verbal abuse: The warning sign in these cases may be bruises. Perhaps the older person reports being afraid of a caregiver or is very anxious about being left alone with him or her.

Neglect and Self-neglect: In these cases, a caregiver is not providing the basic support the older person needs.

It's important to note an older person who is still living independently might be deteriorating because of self-neglect. Suspicions of this may also be reported to APS.

Warning signs would include inadequate food in the house, unclean or unsanitary living conditions, and a lack of medical or dental care.

Exploitation: This is the use of a person's resources or finances without that person's permission. Simply put, it's taking advantage of the older person through force, fear, or deception. A warning sign would be sudden, unexplained losses of money or valuables. It could also take the form of an uninvited guest moving in with the older person.

Abandonment: This is when a caregiver suddenly walks out without giving anyone notice. (Or, in some recently publicized "granny dumping" cases, drops the elderly person at a hospital emergency room entrance and disappears.)

A warning sign within a neighborhood might be realizing a primary caregiver for an elderly person is suddenly gone.

What can a concerned person do? Contact APS through the Area Agency on Aging. You will be asked to supply basic facts and your suspicions. You don't need to prove anything. APS will send a staff person to the site in a timely manner. It recommends you do not investigate the situation yourself.

Of course, filing a false report is never appropriate or justified.

What if you just aren't sure? Call APS. Talk to a professional. Remember, this isn't a case of "Big Brother" spying. It is a part of accepting the Christian responsibility of being our brother's and our sister's keepers.

C. Prayers and How to Say the Rosary

The Sign of the Cross

In the name of the Father, and of the Son, and of the Holy Spirit. Amen.

(To make the Sign of the Cross, the right hand touches the forehead when saying "Father," the chest when saying "Son," the left shoulder when saying "Holy" and the right shoulder when saying "Spirit.")

The Our Father, The Lord's Prayer

Our Father, who art in heaven, hallowed be thy name. Thy kingdom come; thy will be done on earth as it is in heaven. Give us this day our daily bread; and forgive us our trespasses as we forgive those who trespass against us; and lead us not into temptation, but deliver us from evil. Amen.

The Hail Mary

Hail, Mary, full of grace, the Lord is with you; blessed are you among women, and blessed is the fruit of your womb, Jesus. Holy Mary, Mother of God, pray for us sinners, now and at the hour of our death. Amen.

The Glory Be

Glory be to the Father, and to the Son, and to the Holy Spirit. As it was in the beginning, is now, and ever shall be, world without end. Amen.

The Apostles' Creed

I believe in God, the Father almighty, creator of heaven and earth. And in Jesus Christ, his only Son, Our Lord; who was conceived by the Holy Spirit, born of the Virgin Mary, suffered under Pontius Pilate, was crucified, died and was buried. He descended into hell; on the third day he rose again from the dead; He ascended into heaven and sits at the right hand of God the Father almighty; from thence he shall come to judge the living and the dead. I believe in the Holy Spirit, the holy Catholic Church, the communion of saints, the forgiveness of sins, the resurrection of the body, and life everlasting. Amen.

Hail Holy Queen

Hail Holy Queen, Mother of Mercy, our life, our sweetness and our hope. To you do we cry, poor banished children of Eve; to you do we send up our sighs, mourning and weeping in the valley of tears. Turn, then, most gracious advocate, your eyes of mercy toward us, and after this, our exile, show unto us the blessed fruit of your womb, Jesus. O clement, O loving, O sweet Virgin Mary. Pray for us, O holy Mother of God. That we may be made worthy of the promises of Christ.

Let us pray. O God, whose only begotten Son, by his life, death and resurrection, has purchased for us the rewards of eternal life, grant, we beseech You, that meditating on these mysteries in the most holy rosary of the Blessed Virgin Mary, we may imitate what they contain, and obtain what they promise, through the same Christ, our Lord. Amen.

Prayer to One's Guardian Angel

Angel of God, my guardian dear, to whom God's love commits me here, ever this day (night) be at my side, to light, to guard, to rule and guide. Amen.

Prayer of St. Francis

Lord, make me an instrument of your peace.

Where there is hatred let me sow your love

Where there is injury, pardon

Where there is doubt, faith

Where there is despair, hope

Where there is darkness, light

Where there is sadness, joy.

O Divine Master,

Grant that I may not so much seek

to be consoled as to console

to be understood as to understand

to be loved as to love.

For it is in giving that we receive

it is in pardoning that we are pardoned

it is in dying that we are born to eternal life.

The Memorare of St. Bernard

Remember, O most gracious Virgin Mary, that never was it known that anyone who fled to your protection, implored your help, or sought your intercession was left unaided. Inspired by this confidence we fly unto you, O Virgin of virgins, our Mother; to you we come, before you we stand, sinful and sorrowful. O Mother of the Word Incarnate, despise not our petitions, but in your mercy hear and answer them. Amen.

The Act of Contrition

O my God, I am heartily sorry for having offended You, and I detest all my sins because I dread the loss of heaven and the pains of hell, but most of all because they offend You, my God, who are all-good and deserving of all my love. I firmly resolve with the help of your grace to confess my sins, to do penance and to amend my life. Amen.

To Say the Rosary

"Saying a Rosary" usually means reciting five decades — or sets of ten — of Hail Marys. (An entire rosary is fifteen decades.) For each decade there is a "mystery," an event that is meditated on.

The Rosary begins with the Sign of the Cross, the Apostles' Creed, an Our Father, three Hail Marys, and a Glory Be. Each decade is an Our Father, ten Hail Marys, and a Glory Be. It concludes with the Hail Holy Queen.

The joyful mysteries are:
1. The annunciation
2. The visitation
3. The birth of Jesus
4. The presentation of Jesus in the temple
5. The finding of Jesus in the temple

(These are usually said on Sunday from Advent to Lent and on Mondays and Thursdays.)

The sorrowful mysteries are:
1. The agony in the garden
2. The scourging at the pillar
3. The crowning of thorns
4. The carrying of the cross
5. The crucifixion

(These are usually said on Sunday during Lent and on Tuesdays and Fridays.)

The glorious mysteries are:
1. The Resurrection
2. The Ascension
3. The descent of the Holy Spirit on the apostles
4. The Assumption of Mary
5. The coronation of Mary in heaven

(These are usually said on Sunday from Easter to Advent and on Wednesdays and Saturdays.)

Prayer to the Holy Spirit

Come Holy Spirit, fill the hearts of your faithful and enkindle in them the fire of your love. Send forth your Spirit and they shall be created. And You shall renew the face of the earth. Let us pray. O God, who by the light of the Holy Spirit, did instruct the hearts of the faithful, grant that by that same Spirit, we may be truly wise, and ever rejoice in your consolation. Through Christ our Lord. Amen.

D. To Contact the Authors

Monica and Bill Dodds can be contacted in care of: Our Sunday Visitor, 200 Noll Plaza, Huntington, IN 46750. Their e-mail address is: 103362.3330@CompuServe.com. Monica is available to speak to groups on taking care of aging parents.

Our Sunday Visitor...
Your Source for Discovering the Riches of the Catholic Faith

Our Sunday Visitor has an extensive line of materials for young children, teens, and adults. Our books, Bibles, booklets, CD-ROMs, audios, and videos are available in bookstores worldwide.

To receive a FREE full-line catalog or for more information, call **Our Sunday Visitor** at **1-800-348-2440**. Or write, **Our Sunday Visitor** / 200 Noll Plaza / Huntington, IN 46750.

Please send me: __ A catalog
Please send me materials on:
    __ Apologetics and catechetics   __ Reference works
    __ Prayer books   __ Heritage and the saints
    __ The family   __ The parish

Name_____
Address_____Apt._____
City_____State___Zip_____
Telephone (   )_____

                                           A73BBABP

Please send a friend: __ A catalog
Please send a friend materials on:
    __ Apologetics and catechetics   __ Reference works
    __ Prayer books   __ Heritage and the saints
    __ The family   __ The parish

Name_____
Address_____Apt._____
City_____State___Zip_____
Telephone (   )_____

                                           A73BBABP

Our Sunday Visitor
200 Noll Plaza
Huntington, IN 46750
1-800-348-2440
OSVSALES@AOL.COM

Your Source for Discovering the Riches of the Catholic Faith